The Attercliffe Village Trail

Sheffield East End History Trail 2

Text

Ruth Harman and Simon Ogden

Illustrations

Norah K. Rogerson

The **Hallamshire** Press 1997

COVER SHOWS HUNTSMAN WORKS, WORKSOP ROAD, EARLY 19TH CENTURY WITH CRUCIBLE SHOPS ON RIGHT, CEMENTATION FURNACES LEFT CENTRE AND THE OWNER'S HOUSE AND GARDENS.

Doorway, Royal Bank of Scotland, Attercliffe Road

THE ATTERCLIFFE VILLAGE TRAIL

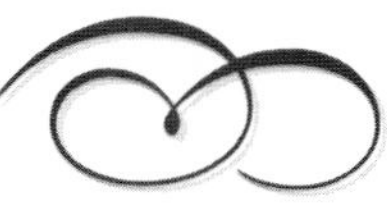

Sheffield East End History Trail 2

Published by The Hallamshire Press
The Hallamshire Press is an imprint of
Interleaf Productions Limited
Broom Hall
8–10 Broomhall Road
Sheffield S10 2DR
UK

Typeset by Interleaf Productions Limited
Printed in Spain by Edelvives

British Library Cataloguing in Publication Data
A catalogue record for this book is available from the British Library

ISBN 1 874718 31 8

Contents

Illustration: Detail from former Coach & Horses Pub, Attercliffe Road

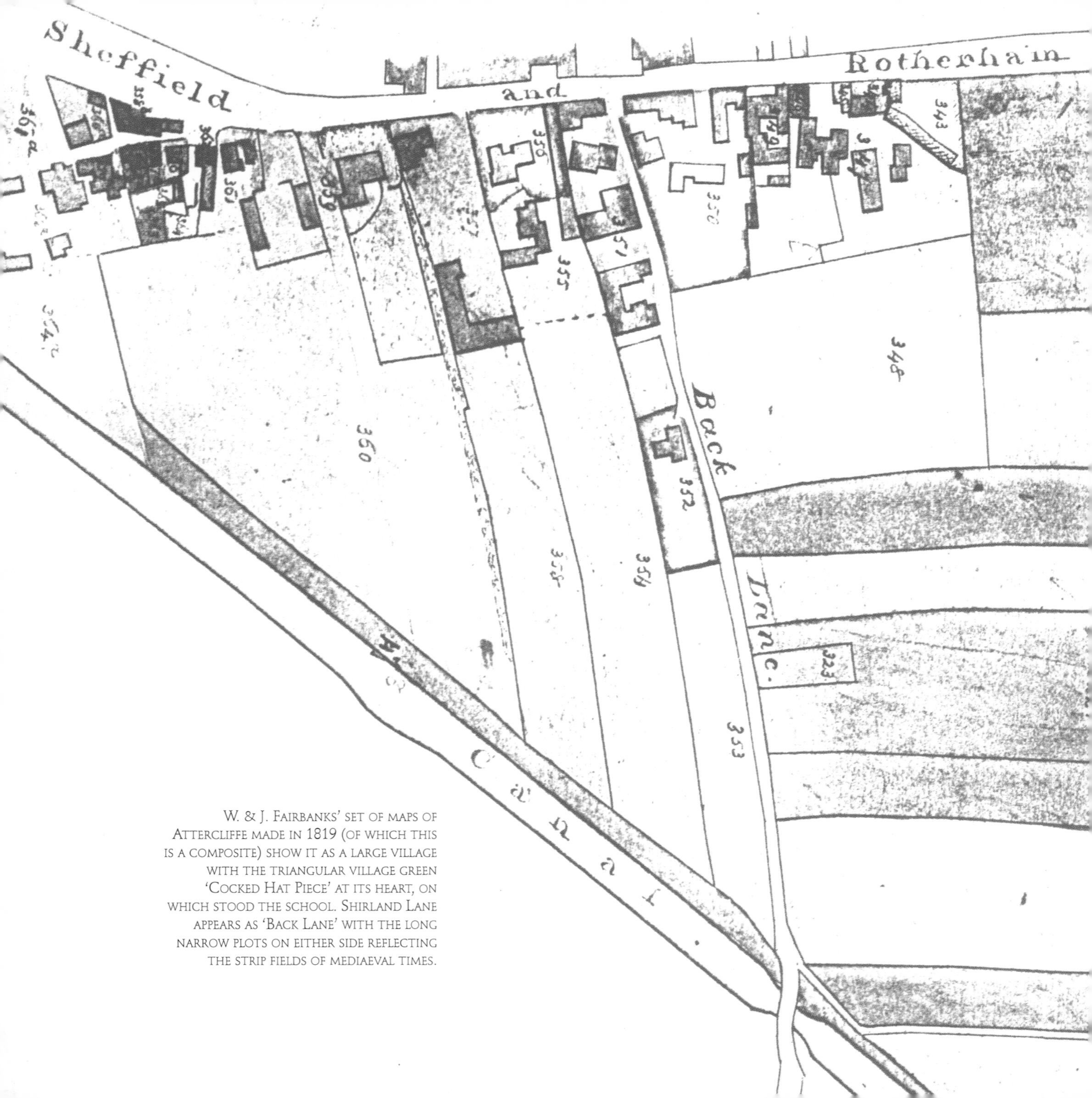

W. & J. Fairbanks' set of maps of Attercliffe made in 1819 (of which this is a composite) show it as a large village with the triangular village green 'Cocked Hat Piece' at its heart, on which stood the school. Shirland Lane appears as 'Back Lane' with the long narrow plots on either side reflecting the strip fields of mediaeval times.

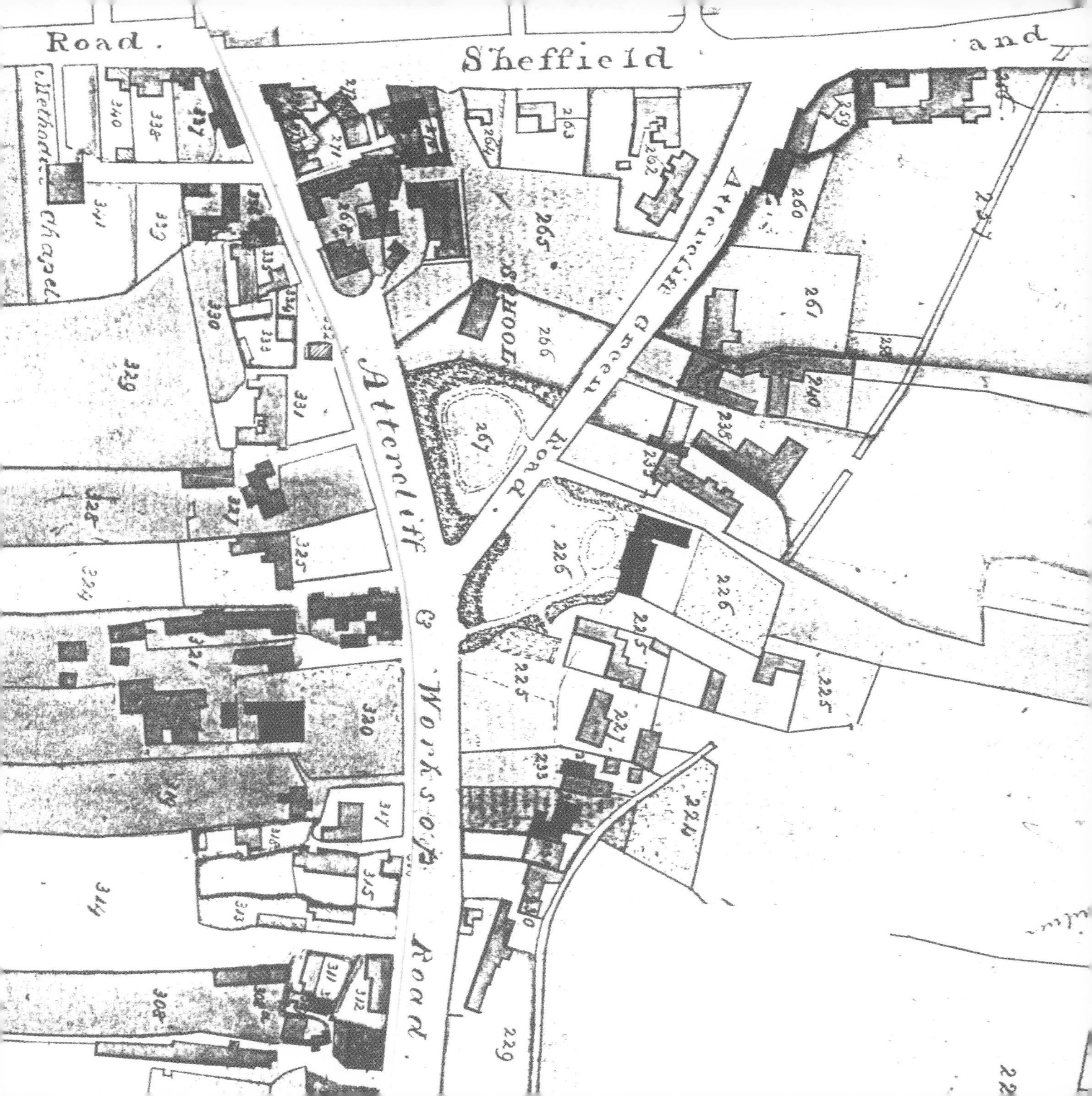

Road. Sheffield and

Methodist Chapel

Attercliff & Worksop Road

Attercliffe Green Road

SCHOOL

340 338 337 341 339 336 335 334 333 332 331 330 329 328 327 325 324 321 320 318 317 316 315 314 313 312 311 308

272 271 270 268 264 263 262 265 266 267 261 260 259 258 240 238 235 226 225 227 224 233 230 229

The Attercliffe Village Trail
To City Centre
River Don
Washford Bridge
1
Staniforth Road
To Darnall
2
Newhall Road
Hilltop Chapel
Attercliffe Road
3
4
To Rotherham
Don Valley Stadium
Sheffield and Tinsley Canal
Worksop Road

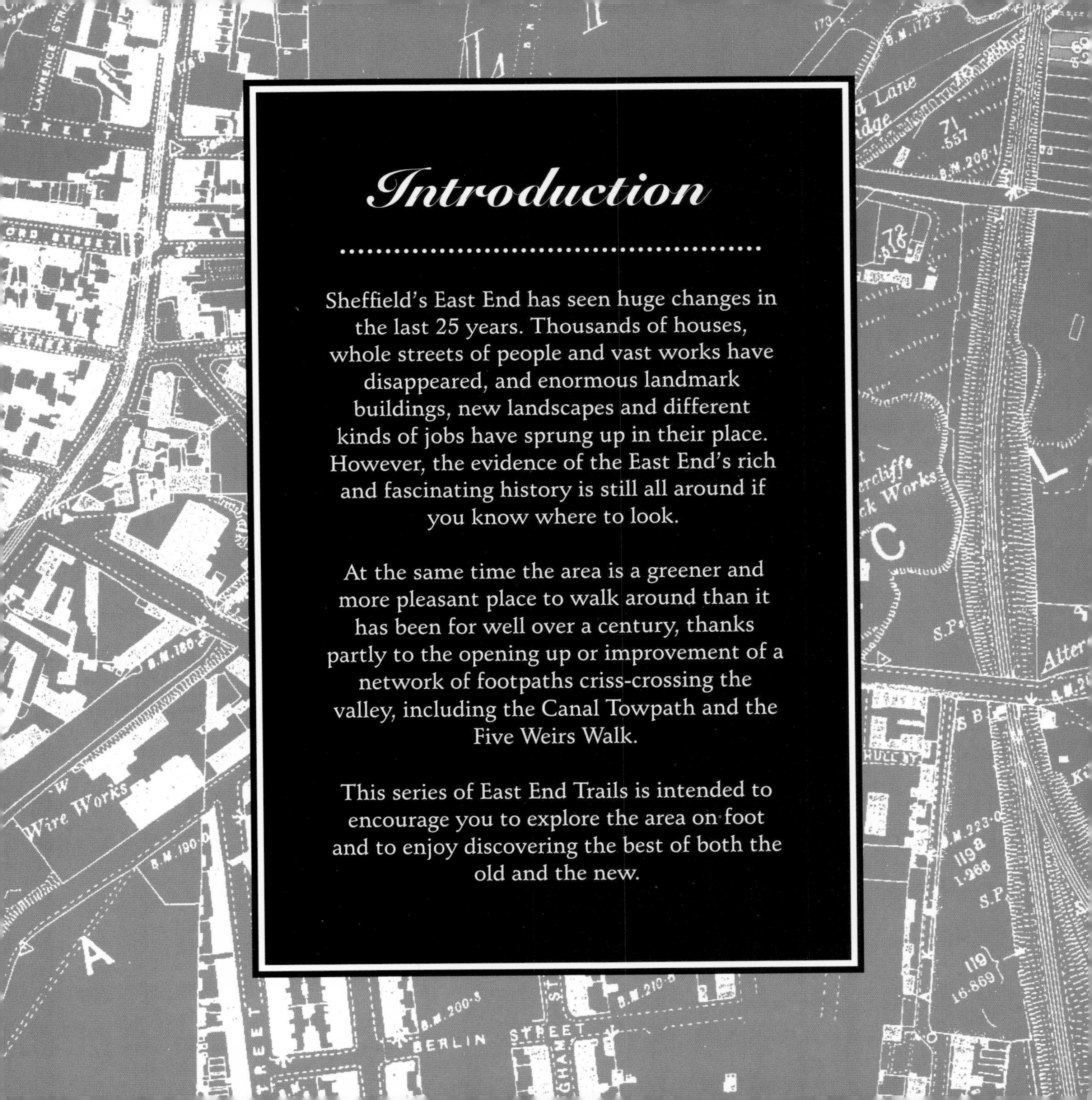

Introduction

Sheffield's East End has seen huge changes in the last 25 years. Thousands of houses, whole streets of people and vast works have disappeared, and enormous landmark buildings, new landscapes and different kinds of jobs have sprung up in their place. However, the evidence of the East End's rich and fascinating history is still all around if you know where to look.

At the same time the area is a greener and more pleasant place to walk around than it has been for well over a century, thanks partly to the opening up or improvement of a network of footpaths criss-crossing the valley, including the Canal Towpath and the Five Weirs Walk.

This series of East End Trails is intended to encourage you to explore the area on foot and to enjoy discovering the best of both the old and the new.

View of Christ Church, Attercliffe Parish Church, from the banks of the Don, c.1845 by I. Shaw. Even in the mid-nineteenth century the Don was still a fishing river. The low 'cliff' on which Attercliffe stands can clearly be seen. Today it is covered in bricks and concrete and the river's course has been changed, but fish, plants and wildlife are coming back.

Why Attercliffe?

This trail is about the transformation of Attercliffe, from pretty country village to one of the most powerful industrial centres in the world, its decline and its current regeneration.

Other parts of Sheffield have also seen such change, but none so dramatic as Attercliffe. Since the early 1960s its population has fallen from over 10,000 down to a mere 300. Over the same period jobs have more than halved from 45,000 down to 18,000, and then climbed back to 30,000.

The trail is not a comprehensive history (see Vine's *The Story of Old Attercliffe* or Farnsworth's *East Enders* for this) but is intended to encourage people actually to visit the area on foot, read the surviving buildings as part of a fascinating story, and to appreciate the now steadily improving environment of the Lower Don Valley, which is once again a place of recreation as well as of work.

The name 'Ateclive' appears in Doomsday and is generally believed to mean 'at the cliff'. The cliff still exists though few people today are aware of it. Generally however, one of Attercliffe's most important features was its flatness in the wide Lower Don Valley in comparison to generally hilly Sheffield, two miles away.

Little is recorded of the tiny settlement until the 17th century although we do know that in 1587 two water powered iron forges existed there belonging to George Talbot, Earl of Shrewsbury (the jailer of Mary, Queen of Scots). One of these sites is today occupied by Sanderson Kayser's Newhall Road Works. 'Attercliffe cum Darnall' was the term usually used for administrative purposes for the small township until the 20th century.

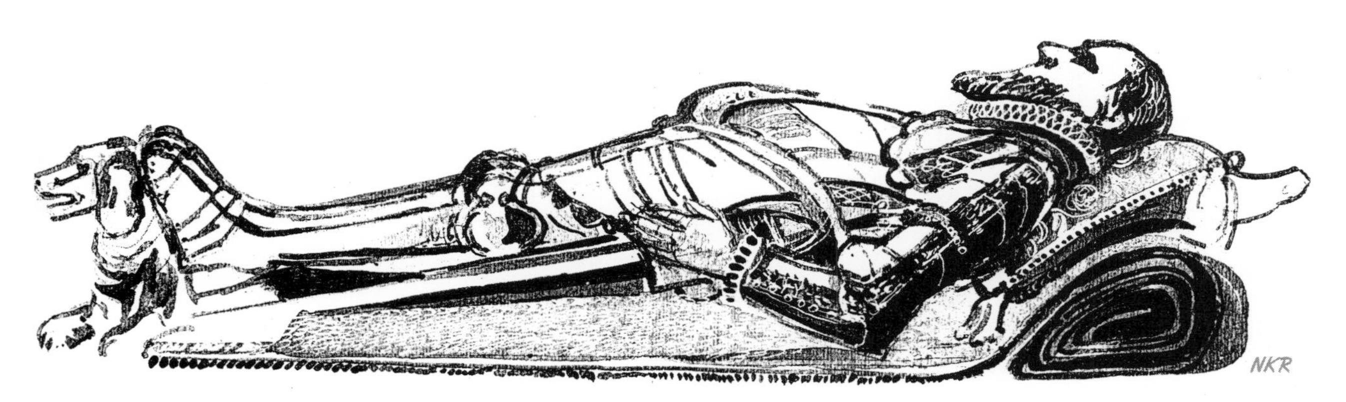

George Talbot, 6th Earl of Shrewsbury (died 1590), is buried in Sheffield Cathedral beneath a sumptuous carved monument.

The Dissenting Tradition

During the Civil War several local families rose to prominence as pillars of the Parliamentary and Protestant cause—the Brights of Carbrook Hall, the Spencers of Attercliffe Old Hall and the Copleys of Attercliffe Forge. From that time began a tradition of religious and political dissent in Sheffield which still influences the city today.

Attercliffe was frequently at the forefront of this movement. In 1629 Hilltop Chapel became the first permanent Anglican place of worship in the Valley. Following the Restoration, the turbulent Matthew Bloom, a curate of Attercliffe, was ejected from the Anglican Church for defying Charles II's Act of Uniformity. He set up the first dissenting chapel in 1678, probably in Staniforth Road. In 1691, 200 years before the beginning of Sheffield University, Attercliffe had its own nationally famous Christ's College, educating 'dissenters' excluded from Oxford and Cambridge by the Act of Uniformity.

The Reverend Richard Frankland (1630–98), a dissenting priest who was ejected from his parish after the Restoration came to Attercliffe in 1686 to found the Dissenting Academy in Attercliffe Old Hall

When the industrial revolution took off in Attercliffe so did non-conformity. Despite four new Anglican parish churches, by 1890 these were easily outnumbered by at least ten substantial chapels in and around Attercliffe. The Victorian chapels often served as a training ground for local politicians, especially of the left, and for trades unionists. Sheffield's first Labour MP, Joe Pointer was elected for Attercliffe in 1909 and socialist organisations like the Independent Labour Party, Social Democratic Federation and later the Communist Party all had strong branches. In the '20s and '30s, Annie Cree and the Communist master-baker George fletcher, led a large unemployed workers movement in the East End. Finally, it was leading Labour Councillors born and bred in the East End who led the calls for massive slum clearance of houses below the 'smoke line' in the 1960s, which resulted in the dismantling of the old East End community.

Joe Pointer, Sheffield & Attercliffe's first Labour MP was elected in 1909.

George Fletcher (1890–1958), popular Communist Leader and founder of Fletcher's Bakeries

The Industrial Revolution

Against this background it is not surprising that Attercliffe's first and most important industrial pioneer, Benjamin Huntsman, was a staunch Quaker. He built his first commercial crucible furnace there in 1751 and thus laid the foundation of the modern steel industry and Sheffield's predominance in it for over two centuries. Huntsman's invention did not, however, immediately transform the village. Not until the area became more accessible through innovations in transport did that occur.

In 1806 Attercliffe could still be described in idyllic terms—'the village is studded with plantations and orchards, and fruit trees overhang the footpath in many parts of the main street', whilst, 'the immediate surroundings are those of rural beauty'.

Most villages around Sheffield specialised in the small scale manufacture of tools or cutlery combined with farming. The speciality of Attercliffe was scissors, but it also had a pottery, a glass works and several small coal mines on the Common.

Developments in transport were soon to bring rapid change. The turnpiking of Attercliffe Road and Worksop Road confirmed Attercliffe as the centre for the valley and a significant stage coach stop (note the pub names: Coach and Horses [now the 'Safari Guest House']; The Travellers). The Sheffield and Tinsley Canal, opened in 1819, passed through the village and brought cheap coal from South Yorkshire and Swedish iron, as well as providing a convenient outlet for Sheffield-

The newly industrialised East End c.1879 with Scotia Works in the foreground and Park Iron Works (now Tempered Spring) beyond the river on what is now Leveson Street. Attercliffe Road Station can be seen on the far right of this picture.

made products. Now steam powered factories began to line the canal banks from Attercliffe to Sheffield, and new coal mines were opened at Tinsley Park, Attercliffe and Sheffield Park (see Trail 1 on the Canal).

Anticipation of the canal encouraged the Enclosure by Act of Parliament of 280 acres of common land round the village. As was usually the case, most of the land went to established local landowners and the villagers lost not only the three big medieval fields between Attercliffe and Darnall, but even the ancient village green or 'Cocked Hat Piece'. Lack of opposition was claimed to be due to the absence of many men who were away in Wellington's armies. The local historian Joseph Hunter, called it 'one of the most selfish enclosure acts ever passed.'

The one event which triggered off wholesale development of the valley was the opening of the Sheffield to Rotherham Railway in 1838. New heavy engineering and steel works then started to advance rapidly along the railway between Savile Street and Carlisle Street led by such famous firms as Cammells, Firths, John Browns, Vickers and Spear & Jackson.

The new works and mines created an insatiable demand for labour, sucking in immigrants from even farther away. In 1811 the population of Attercliffe and Darnall was 2,673. By 1872 it was 17,447 and ten years later 26,968. By the end of the armaments boom of the First World War it had reached a peak of 50,000.

In the 1870s Attercliffe became the centre of a vast new industrial suburb where factories and houses were being thrown up in unplanned profusion. 'A few brief moments transforms breathing space into rows of habitations more or less jerry built', regretted the *Attercliffe Almanack* of 1897. In 1873, Sheffield's first horse tram route ran along Attercliffe Road from the town centre.

At first many leading industrialists themselves lived in Attercliffe, notably Joseph Beardshaw, Samuel Jackson, the Huntsmans, Jabez Shipman, Ambrose Shardlow and Joseph Jonas. Several served as Councillors for the area, but as the noise and smoke increased they moved one by one to more rural or suburban surroundings, leaving Attercliffe to their workers.

Between 1870 and 1960 the Lower Don Valley remained one of the classic industrial landscapes of Britain, with some of the worst pollution in the world. Only Pittsburg and Dusseldorf—also steel cities, were considered dirtier. five hundred tons of soot fell on each square mile of the Valley annually. Many former East End housewives recall changing net curtains twice a week. Babies could not safely be left outside.

Drop hammers, rolling mills and coke ovens worked night and day in close proximity to schools and houses. Many dwellings were built back-to-back around courtyards over which towered the steelworks.

Typical two-up, two-down houses with shared yards, Weedon Street 1966

Living Standards

Yet in its heyday Attercliffe was also a great centre of working class sport and entertainment and a shopping centre second only to the city centre itself. On Attercliffe Road alone in the 1930s there were 26 clothes shops, 15 butchers, 11 chip shops, 3 cinemas, a music hall and 40 pubs!

With so many men engaged in hot work in the forges and foundries, beer drinking on the shop floor was standard practice before 1914. Pubs opened at 6.00am for men coming off night shift, and the heavy drinking naturally continued on Saturday nights. The stage was set for a classic confrontation between Temperance, supported strongly by the nonconformist chapels (and many early socialists) and the Demon Drink. As well as pubs, Attercliffe boasted quite a number of temperance bars and cafes.

Steelworkers were always under threat of spells of unemployment or short time if trade was poor, but the East End saw its hardest times in the 1920s and 1930s with the long miners' strike followed by depression and mass unemployment. Many households came

ATTERCLIFFE ROAD/STANIFORTH ROAD CORNER, EARLY 20TH CENTURY

close to starvation and the spectacle of barefoot children begging stale bread—'bread-lefting'—from bakers was common. Yet out of that shared hardship was forged a community where neighbour helped neighbour and doors were never locked. Thousands who left the East End when slum clearance started found, too late, that such communities could not easily be rebuilt.

Street Party, VE Day—Sleaford Street, Attercliffe

The Fall and Rise of Attercliffe

After World War Two prosperity returned to Attercliffe for some 30 years. New demands for labour drew workers from the Caribbean, the Yemen and the Indian sub-continent. The Asians in particular came to regard Attercliffe as the centre of their community, and their shops, restaurants, banks, mosques and a cinema became a feature of Attercliffe Road. Attercliffe is still a noted centre for Asian restaurants and businesses.

By this time, however, the slum clearance programme had got underway and one after another the terraced streets disappeared under the bulldozer. Even with most of the residents gone, the shops and pubs on Attercliffe Road hung on, until the works closures of the 1980s proved the final straw for many.

In the '60s and '70s the Council planned that land in the East End vacated by slum clearance would be used for industry to expand. In some cases this happened, but in the late '70s when the clearance was almost complete, a decline in the steel industry began and soon many of the great works were themselves vacant sites. By 1985 over one third of the Valley was derelict, drawing comparison with the worst of the Blitz.

STEEL MELTERS AT BROWN BAYLEY'S, EARLY 20TH CENTURY

Rather than one vast heavy industrial estate, a new vision of the East End has been developed, first by the Council and then by Sheffield Development Corporation. In this vision the Valley has regained some of its former greenness and beauty with a cleaner river and canal and areas of trees and grass. Within this setting activities like sport, leisure and shopping have come back to the area, side by side with both established and modern 'high tech' industry. Now housing is coming back to Attercliffe, supported by a strong local campaign.

The Valley is far more attractive than at any time for a century and new buildings have risen from the dereliction. Yet even the return of activity has sometimes brought the demolition of more familiar landmarks. All the more reason to make sure that the history of the area is not forgotten or obliterated, but adds to its richness and interest.

The Old Blue Bell pub, Worksop Road, now the Quba Mosque

SECTION ONE

WASHFORD BRIDGE TO STANIFORTH ROAD

The trail begins at Washford Bridge (1), where the River Don, which forms the boundary between Attercliffe and Brightside, swings north-west in a great tree-lined curve before resuming its north-easterly course a little further downstream. When Attercliffe was still a village this area was fields, through which passed the ancient route from Sheffield to Tinsley and Rotherham, now Attercliffe Road.

Washford Bridge, built in 1794 to replace two older ones nearby, carries Attercliffe Road across the river. Although it has been altered, its three arches, constructed of large ashlar blocks of honey-coloured sandstone, are an impressive sight.

To the south of the road. a little before the bridge, is the former Salmon Pastures school (2), a rather plain stone building built for the Education Committee in 1908. Its name commemorates the meadows which lay in the loop of the river and the fact that salmon were, in less polluted times, caught in the Don. The garage on the corner of Warren Street stands on the site of Emmanuel Church, consecrated in 1882 for a new parish in this area and bombed in 1940.

At the traffic lights turn left into Stevenson Road, then left again into Birch Road and Bessemer Place. Bessemer Place, which has stone setts as its road surface, is named after Sir Henry Bessemer (1813–98), who helped perfect the method of making high-quality steel in large quantities, an invention that led directly to the development of the great steel works in the valley. Between it and Birch Road is the former Manager's House for Attercliffe Corn Mill, which stood to the right between Birch and Stevenson Roads, and was in existence as a steam mill by 1805. The miller's house, which then stood in spacious grounds surrounded by fields, has two canted bays and a curiously modest off-centre entrance. Possibly this and the assymetrical roof indicate that the present front of smooth sandstone blocks is the result of the later extension and refacing of the original house. The mill itself was twice

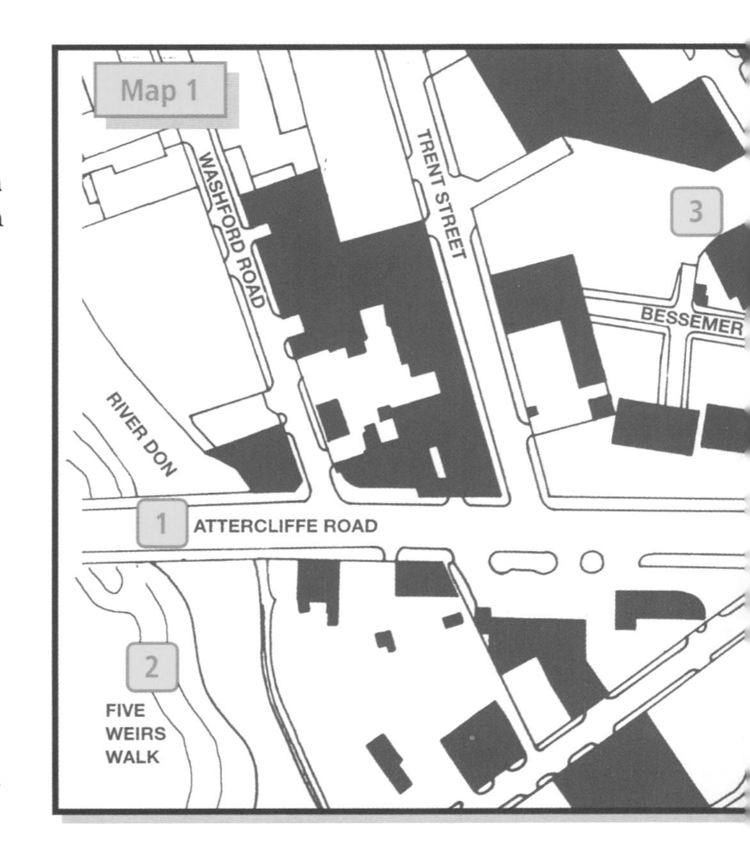

destroyed by fire, in 1805, when it was rebuilt, and again in 1863. After this the house was used for many years as a Dispensary, where by paying a penny a week members could obtain medical attention and medicines, and later became the home of the Foundry Workers Club and Institute, and then the first Caribbean Social Club in the city.

Carrying on, note the shop opposite Stevenson Road (4), formerly a temperance bar. A large painted sign used to proclaim 'Try our Sarsaparilla and Herb Beer Tonic' and 'Herbs, Roots, Barks in Stock', a reminder that the current interest in natural herbal remedies is nothing new. Nearby, in Armstead Road, which no longer exists, were the Attercliffe Turkish Baths which in 1888 claimed to offer 'The best sixpenny Turkish Bath in England'. In the 1920s a shop here on Attercliffe Road served as the headquarters of the Communist Party and was known jokingly as 'the Smolny'—after the Russian Bolsheviks' first H.Q.

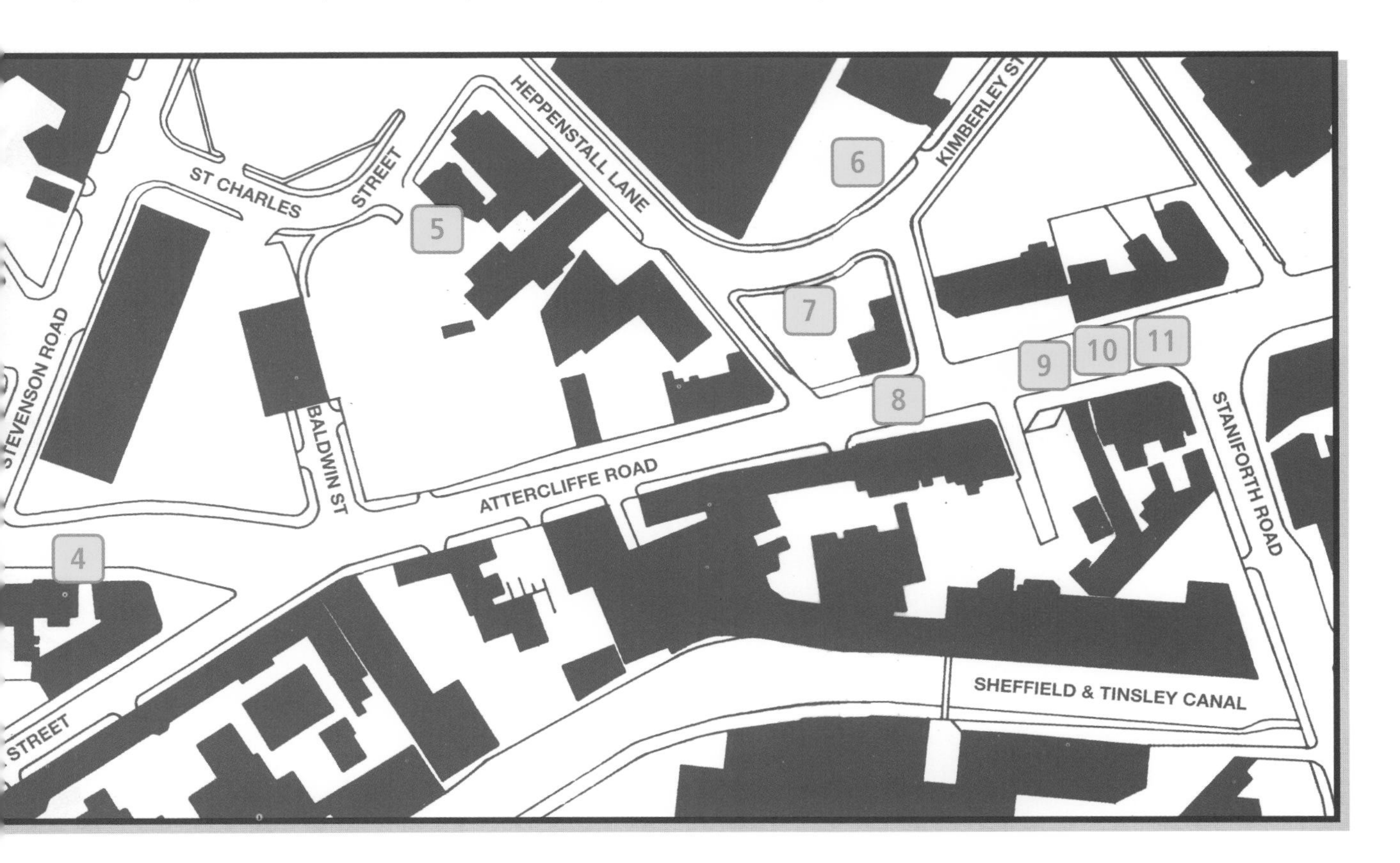

Washford Bridge, 1889

A little way along Stevenson Road turn right into St Charles Street. Here the Roman Catholic Church of St Charles Borromeo (5), which, together with the adjoining presbytery, was built in 1876, is now the only church in Attercliffe retaining its original form and use. The buildings were designed by the Sheffield architects C.J. Innocent and T.B. Brown, and largely paid for by the 15th Duke of Norfolk, one of the major landowners in Attercliffe and a leading Catholic. Architecturally, the church is quite simple with five two-light windows in the nave and a small bell turret, all built in coursed rubble-faced stone.

Next door in Heppenstall Lane is the former church school, a rather severe and angular building, built in 1929 as a plaque records, to replace an earlier one of 1871. Like the church it was built on a very constricted site and has a roof-top playground. Most of the open space which now serves as a car park was occupied by terraced houses until the 1960s.

Just before you reach Attercliffe Road again you will pass, over on the left, the site of Carlton House (6). It was built in the 18th century in pleasant grounds. In the middle of the last century it was the home of Samuel Jackson, co-founder of the famous firm of Spear & Jackson, manufacturers of saws, files and edge tools whose works were on Savile Street. The length of Attercliffe Road from Washford Bridge to Colwall Street was for many years known as Carlton Road and the Carlton Pub on Attercliffe Road preserves the name.

SECTION ONE

On Heppenstall Lane itself there was a small terrace of three handsome houses (7) dated 1779 which, although listed, became very derelict resulting in their unfortunate demolition in 1987. Jabez Shipman (1823–93), another local industrialist and councillor for Attercliffe from 1870 to 1883, lived here for a time, facing his steel works and wire mills, founded in 1860 with Robert Hadfield, across Attercliffe Road. Now called the Spartan Works (8), the long range with its archway, leading to a yard and workshops behind, is typical of a Victorian steelworks and is notable for the decorative bricks used over the windows and below the string course (see detail at the foot of the pages).

Turn left and walk a little farther up Attercliffe Road. Opposite are the offices and works of Messrs Hartley and Son (9), the local printers and stationers, whose *Attercliffe Almanack* issued between 1880 and 1898 is a mine of local information.

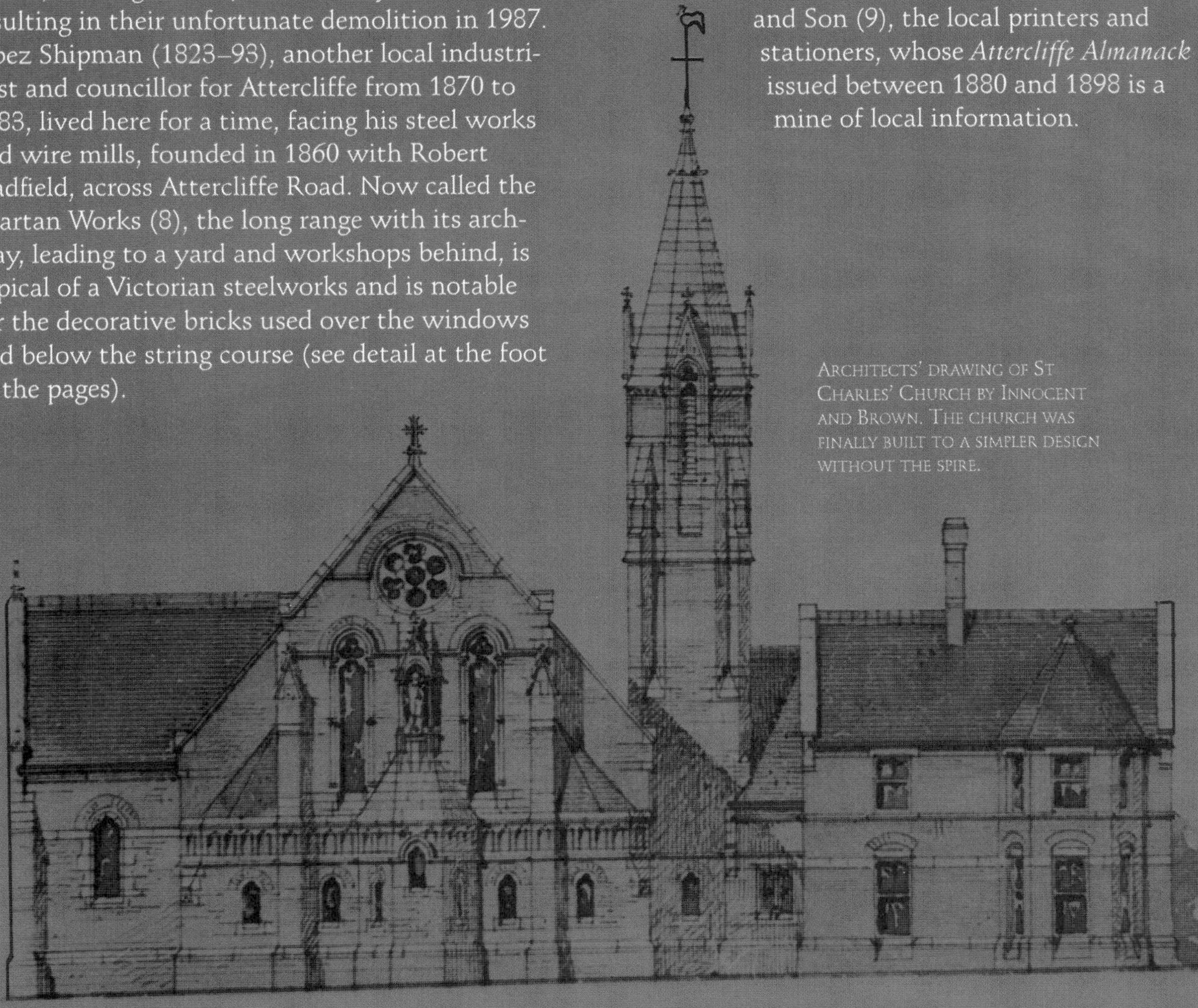

Architects' drawing of St Charles' Church by Innocent and Brown. The church was finally built to a simpler design without the spire.

The former Trustee Savings Bank (10) next door was originally a branch of the Sheffield Savings Bank and was built in 1899–1900. Similar to the main bank in Norfolk Street and the branch at Heeley, its sandstone front of three bays is in a simple classical style with tall round arched windows.

On the corner is the Yorkshire Bank (11), originally the Yorkshire Penny Bank, as indicated by the initials 'PYB' in the shaped gable above the main entrance. The building, faced in yellow sandstone, was completed in 1905. Notice the decoration of children's' heads set among fruit between the ground floor windows, and peeping out from behind the capitals beside the door—perhaps these were intended to encourage even the youngest to start the habit of saving, for the penny banks were founded specifically for people with only very small sums to deposit.

Carlton House from Kimberley Street, 1930s

Details from
Yorkshire
(Penny) Bank

SECTION TWO

STANIFORTH ROAD TO WORKSOP ROAD

Cross over Attercliffe Road at the traffic lights, and walk up Staniforth Road to the bridge over the canal (12). This was originally Pinfold Bridge, built when the canal was made in 1815–19 to carry a lane which eventually dwindled away among the fields towards Darnall. Here, to the south of the village, were the three great medieval open fields of Attercliffe, named in Harrison's survey of 1637 as Crossgate, Dean and Park fields. Fairbank's map of 1795 shows that some long narrow strips still survived up to the enclosure of the remaining open fields in 1810.

To the south-west of the fields, near the old Woodbourn Road School, now the Pakistan Muslim Centre, once stood Woodbourn Hall, birthplace of Henry Clifton Sorby (1826–1908) whose scientific researches in archaeology, chemistry, geology, metallurgy and natural history brought him international fame. He pioneered the examination of rocks under the microscope and then, more significantly for Sheffield, extended his studies to steel and other metals with far-reaching results. The area around the Hall was later built over with rows of terraced houses but these too have now disappeared and have been replaced by Woodbourn athletics track and new factories.

Staniforth Road used to be called Pinfold Lane after the nearby 'pinfold', an enclosure used for centuries to impound stray animals (caught by the 'pinder' until they were released by their owners on payment of a fine). The lane was extended to Darnall Church in 1891 to become

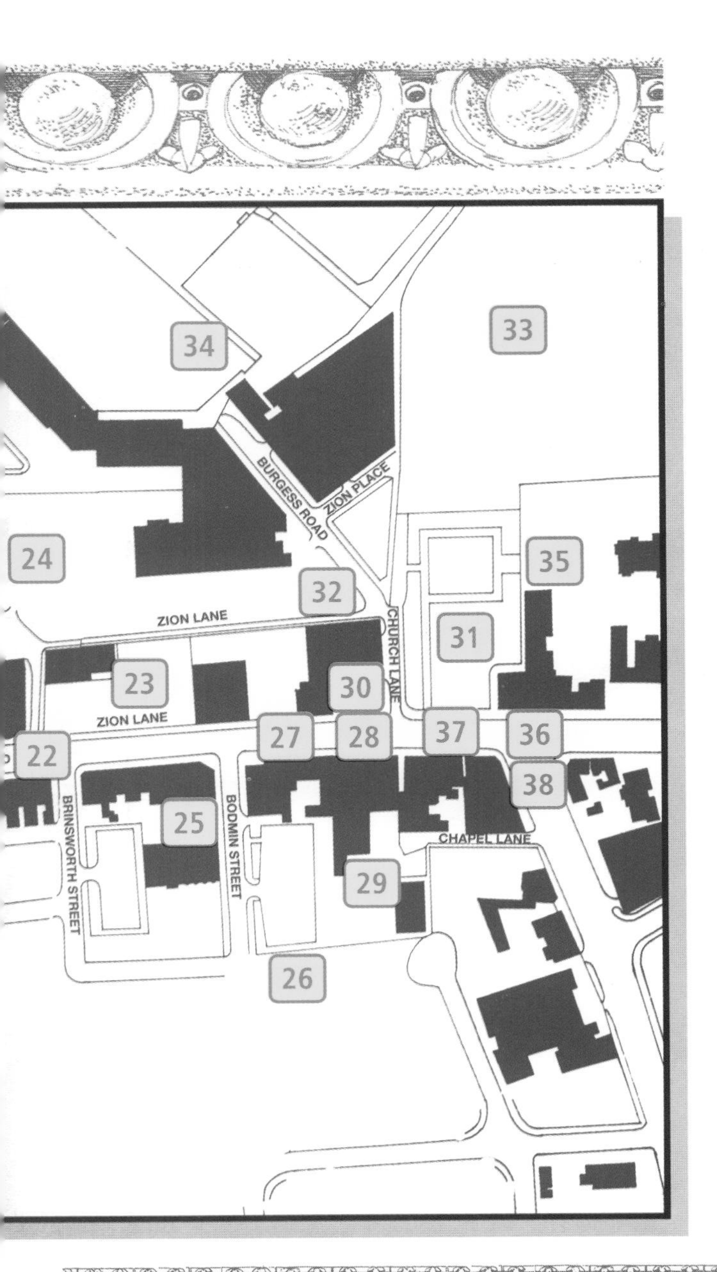

Staniforth Road. Being a tram route it gradually replaced the older turnpike road along Worksop and Darnall Roads as the main link between the two villages. The old bridge over the canal was replaced by a much wider one in 1897, which was widened again in the 1920s, to form the present Pinfold Bridge.

Before you retrace your steps back to Attercliffe Road, stop at the row of shops set back from the road on the right (13). These stand on the site of one of Attercliffe's Victorian theatres, the Theatre Royal, which was built in 1896–7. It could accommodate 700–800 people and, by providing a bill of regular variety performances, was a major addition to the facilities for entertainment available locally at the end of the 19th Century. By the 1930s however, demand had changed and it was reconstructed as the Regal Cinema in 1935. Known latterly as the 'Bug Hut', its popularity declined and it, in turn, eventually suffered the same fate as all but one of Attercliffe's other cinemas, being demolished in the early '60s.

Before continuing to the right on Attercliffe Road look at the shop on the corner (14) which was built as a branch of Montague Burton's in 1931. Faced in white ceramic 'faience' blocks, a hallmark of the Burton's chain of shops built at that period, it retains its original bronze window frames, black marble plinth with ventilation grilles proclaiming 'Montague Burton the Tailor of Taste', and the foundation stone laid by Stanley Howard Burton in 1931 beside the recessed doorway. The first floor was originally the Broadway

Billiard Hall, reached from staircases at either end of the shop fronts, but was converted into the Astoria Dance Hall in 1947. This enjoyed a racy reputation on account of the liveliness of its Saturday night dances! Many Burton's shops were deliberately built with Billiard Halls over—presumably as an extra attraction to potential male customers.

It is not, perhaps, generally realised that Montague Burton (1885–1952), the founder of the firm, originally established his business in Sheffield, before moving to Leeds, where the clothes were actually made. He revolutionised the concept of men's tailoring and brought made-to-measure suits and coats within the reach of the working man, at the sensational price, in 1913, of 30 shillings! From 5 shops (all in the north of England) in 1913, the business had expanded to 200 in 1920, and by 1929 Burton had 400 shops and his own factories making not only clothes but also cloth. An excellent employer, and a pioneer in the field of industrial welfare, Burton maintained that low wages were a false economy and in 1921 claimed he paid the highest wages in the tailoring trade in Europe. He was also a passionate advocate of industrial and international peace, founding a branch of the League of Nations Union for his employees in Leeds in 1922, and endowing University chairs in both industrial and international relations.

Woodbourn Hall, now long demolished

Henry Clifton Sorby, metallurgist and naturalist (1826–1908)

SECTION TWO

St Paul's Methodist New Connexion Chapel, architects' drawing 1868—the chapel was actually surrounded by terraced houses not trees! The site is now a car park.

Opposite Burtons is Oakes Green, now only a street name, but commemorating the fact that this area was, until the Enclosure of 1820, an open green (also known at one time as Beighton Green) with a few cottages around it. It was probably from his wife's family cottage in this area that the great funeral procession of the Chartist, Samuel Holberry, said to have numbered 50,000 set out for the General Cemetery in June 1842.

Further along Attercliffe Road, near the corner of Colwall, formerly Chapel Street, was the site of the first Methodist New Connexion Chapel in Attercliffe, opened in about 1836. This was replaced by a new chapel, St Paul's in Shortridge Street, on the other side of Attercliffe Road, in 1868–69 (demolished in 1978).

The shops opposite Banner's store (15) mark the beginning of the old High Street, and are fairly typical of the three-storey buildings which replaced older, detached houses in gardens and so transformed the appearance of the street in the last quarter of the 19th century, when it was enjoying new-found prosperity. They have some pretension to architectural quality in features like the scroll brackets supporting the lintels over the first floor windows, but are quite over-shadowed by Banner's store (16) which has been one of the most prominent buildings in Attercliffe since it was built in 1933–34, and remains a local land-mark. A large square block of three storeys, it is faced in white faience blocks and is decorated with urns along the top of the parapet. The shop was designed by the local architects, Chapman and Jenkinson, antique dealers for John Banner,

BANNER'S ADVERT FROM *ATTERCLIFFE ALMANACK*

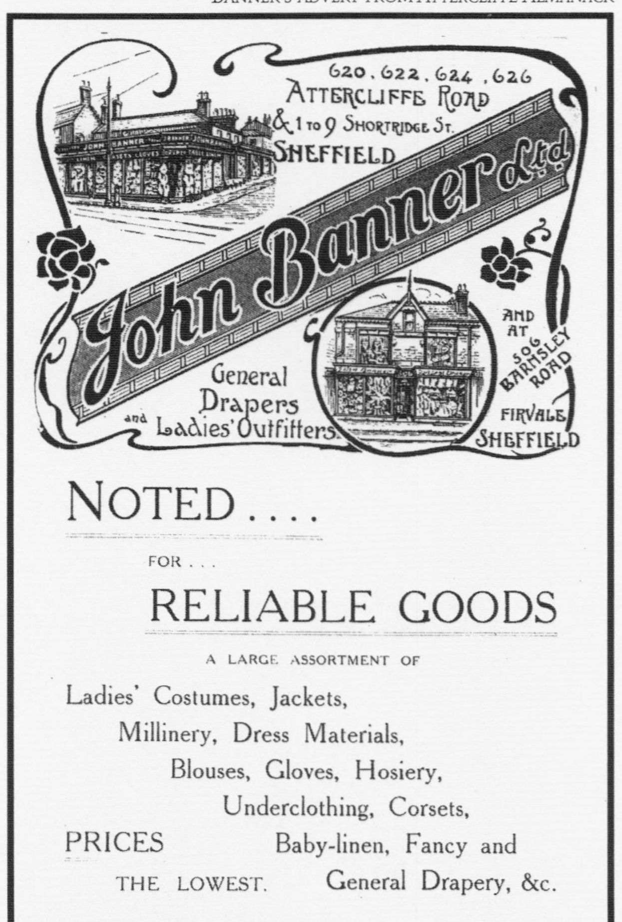

whose original drapery business, founded in 1873, and established here in 1894, had expanded rapidly. John Banner served as a Councillor for Attercliffe and was a prominent member of St Paul's chapel. The store itself closed but the building is still in use, using the Banner's name, and occupied by a variety of smaller retailers and the 'Past Times' museum of wartime Sheffield.

The little building (17) next door on Shortridge Street was built as a Post Office. Its brick front is decorated with features such as the swags on

DETAILS OF FORMER POST OFFICE, SHORTRIDGE STREET

either side of the first floor windows, and the balustrade above them, all made in white faience, similar to that used for Banner's store.

Continue along Attercliffe Road to Shirland Lane, stopping to look at the former Midland Bank (18) opposite on the corner of Baker Street. Formerly a branch of the Sheffield and Hallamshire Bank, it was one of the first large bank buildings in Attercliffe, opening on 4th July, 1892.

Notice the roof especially—its slates are laid in diminishing courses, gradually decreasing in size towards the top. This is a more expensive way of slating a roof, normally only found on larger buildings of quality (for example the Town Hall). Welsh slates of different sizes have their own individual names, including, in ascending order of size, Ladies, Viscountesses, Countesses, Marchionesses, Duchesses, Princesses, Empresses and Queens.

On the other corner of Baker Street stood until recently an imposing block, (19) with large gables, built about 1886 for Dr George Huntsman Shaw, a much loved local doctor, whose father and grandfather had preceded him in the practice. The buildings here included his house and surgery and five shops.

Until some fifteen years ago, Shirland Lane led to an area of densely packed terraced houses, now all demolished, as is the small Unitarian chapel which stood a little way up on the right hand side. Built in 1906, it closed as a chapel in 1971, and was then used as a mosque until this was damaged by fire. Before houses were built, this area formed the grounds of Shirland House, a large early 19th century house which was the home of the Deakin family for many years. Now both it and the later houses have gone and the site has been redeveloped as the Sheffield Industry Business Technology Centre (SIBTEC) (20), to encourage the sort of technical innovation in manufacturing that Benjamin Huntsman brought to the area some 250 years ago.

At the Queens Head pub (21), cross over Attercliffe Road and look at the unexceptional block of modern shops next to it (22), which includes the Don Valley Drop-in Centre. This occupies the site of the famous Attercliffe Palace, opened as the Alhambra Theatre of Varieties on 3rd January 1889, and re-named the Palace Theatre in 1907. Designed by G.D. Martin and A. Blomfield Jackson, the architects of Her Majesty's and the Prince of Wales' theatres in London, it was Attercliffe's second theatre and could seat 1,600 people, plus another 400 standing. The prices for seats in its lavish 'Moorish' interior were one shilling in the orchestra stalls, 6d in the stalls and balcony and 3d for the rest. Amongst the famous names associated with it are Charlie Chaplin, Bud flannagan, Harry Secombe and Beryl Reid, and it played a central role in Attercliffe life for over half a century, managed

'Whit sings', Attercliffe Road, the chapel congregation out in force

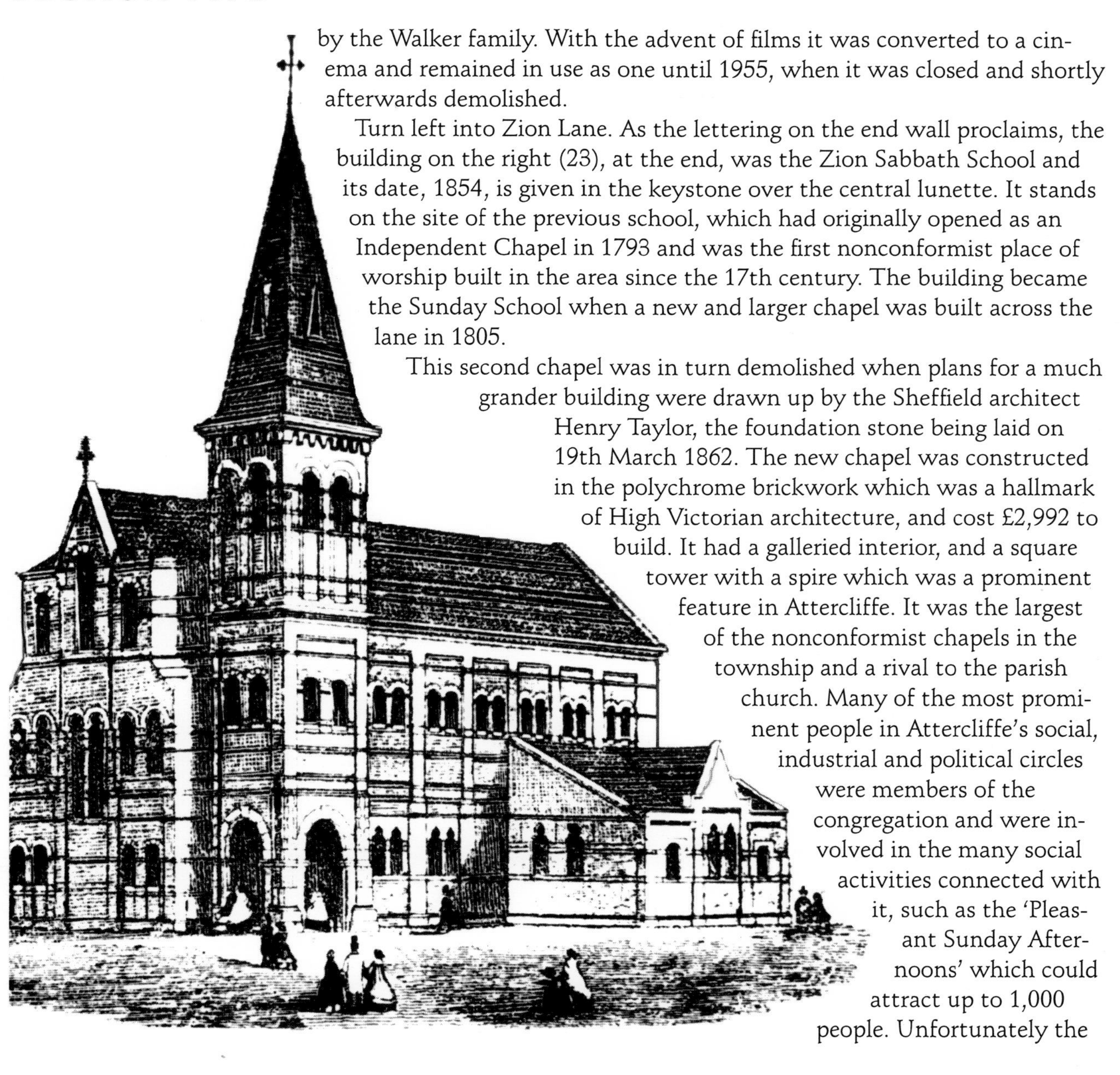

by the Walker family. With the advent of films it was converted to a cinema and remained in use as one until 1955, when it was closed and shortly afterwards demolished.

Turn left into Zion Lane. As the lettering on the end wall proclaims, the building on the right (23), at the end, was the Zion Sabbath School and its date, 1854, is given in the keystone over the central lunette. It stands on the site of the previous school, which had originally opened as an Independent Chapel in 1793 and was the first nonconformist place of worship built in the area since the 17th century. The building became the Sunday School when a new and larger chapel was built across the lane in 1805.

This second chapel was in turn demolished when plans for a much grander building were drawn up by the Sheffield architect Henry Taylor, the foundation stone being laid on 19th March 1862. The new chapel was constructed in the polychrome brickwork which was a hallmark of High Victorian architecture, and cost £2,992 to build. It had a galleried interior, and a square tower with a spire which was a prominent feature in Attercliffe. It was the largest of the nonconformist chapels in the township and a rival to the parish church. Many of the most prominent people in Attercliffe's social, industrial and political circles were members of the congregation and were involved in the many social activities connected with it, such as the 'Pleasant Sunday Afternoons' which could attract up to 1,000 people. Unfortunately the chapel, which had survived closure and was used as a furniture store, was demolished in June 1987 after being badly damaged by fire.

The graveyard behind it (24) still survives, though it is badly neglected and vandalised. Amongst the many local people associated with the chapel were the Read and Wilson families of Royds Mill (now Thessco Ltd) and Wincobank Hall, of whom Mrs Mary Anne Rawson née Read (1807–87) is one of the most notable. She was a founder of the Sheffield Ladies Anti-Slavery Campaign and worked tirelessly for it by writing and speaking and even trying to gain support from every housewife in Sheffield for an early boycott of West Indian Sugar. She is buried in the chapel yard, but unfortunately no headstone now marks her grave. The Wilsons also supplied two Lord Mayors, and Cecil Wilson was Labour MP for Attercliffe in the 1920s.

Before turning to go back to Attercliffe Road, notice the unusual arrangement of sandstone and granite setts in Zion Lane, still unspoilt by later coverings of tarmac. Carts and coaches once rumbled up here to a livery stables, and have worn grooves in the sandstone.

A little further down Attercliffe Road cross over into Bodmin Street, formerly known as Orchard Street, marking the site of the orchard belonging to Attercliffe Old Hall. The street was created in 1854 when a Wesleyan Reform Chapel and Sunday School was built here—the present building (25) opened in 1891 and has been used as a mosque and a Muslim Community Centre since 1967. The chapel's name and date can be seen on a stone plaque in the pediment, while the memorial stones, dated 25th August 1890, are set in the front wall. Among those associated with the chapel were Sir Frederick Thorpe Mappin, Baronet, owner of the Sheaf Works on the Canal, Liberal MP for Hallamshire from 1885 to 1906 and benefactor of the Mappin Art Gallery, and Mrs. Hadfield, widow of the founder of the steel firm, Hadfields.

Further up Bodmin Street on the left was Huntsman's Gardens School (26), built on market gardens once belonging to the Huntsman family. In the 1870s these were apparently noted for the fine rhubarb grown by Henry Titterton, whose

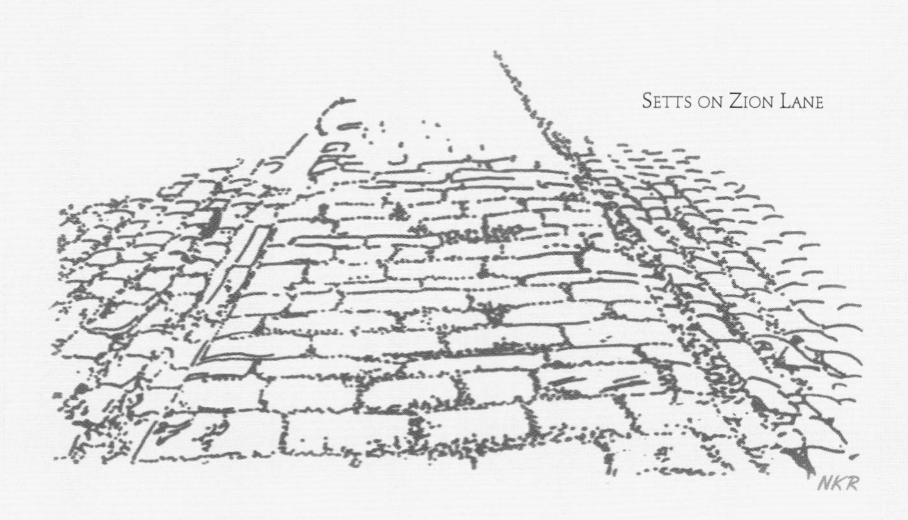

Setts on Zion Lane

name is remembered in Titterton Street. Titterton was a Trades Unionist and Temperance campaigner who did much to fight the practice of paying out wages in pubs. The school, which opened in 1884, was of a novel radial design and was the work of the Sheffield architect, C.J. Innocent. It could accommodate 1,250 pupils, all of whom were visible simultaneously from the Headmaster's desk! George Vine, the noted local historian of Attercliffe, was Headmaster here in the 1920s.

Return to the main road and turn right.

The Station Hotel (27)—an old fashioned pub whose narrow front belies its maze of small rooms, commemorates the long-closed Attercliffe Station (see Section 3). It is said to have been established by Joshua Eyre, who earned his money as a travelling fiddler.

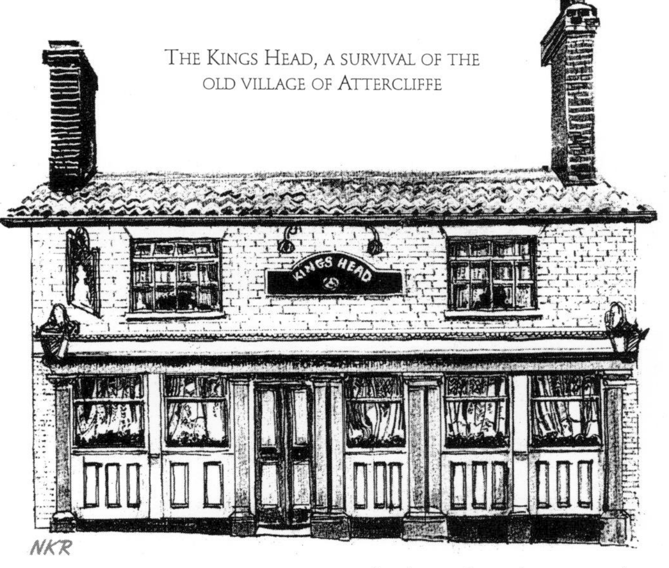

THE KINGS HEAD, A SURVIVAL OF THE OLD VILLAGE OF ATTERCLIFFE

The modern shops including the Post Office (28) stand on the site of yet another of Attercliffe's many nonconformist chapels—the Methodist Meeting House built in 1803 on land given by Thomas Holy, a leading Methodist in Sheffield. The chapel was enlarged in 1824, 1832 and 1883 to cope with its growing congregation, and the Sunday School (29) (now on Chapel Lane) was built behind it in 1875. In 1924 the chapel was closed and demolished to make way for a new Methodist Central Hall, the gravestones and remains from the old chapel yard being removed to Darnall cemetery. In 1965 the Central Hall was itself demolished and replaced by the present shops. This succession of buildings here and at Zion graphically illustrates the meteoric rise and subsequent decline of nonconformity in the area.

The Kings Head pub (30), almost opposite, has an interesting history dating from at least the early 19th Century when it was owned by Robert Jackson, father of the Samuel who co-founded the firm of Spear & Jackson and later lived at Carlton House. Robert ran a grocery and earthenware dealers shop here, and was succeeded in 1839 by John Appleton, chemist and druggist.

The building's most famous occupant, however, was George Littlewood (1859–1912) whose father was licensee when it became a pub. A champion runner and walker of international standing, George Littlewood won many trophies at the 'pedestrian' races so popular in the 1880s and '90s. These took the form of endurance tests rather than specific distance events. Many such events were held in Attercliffe at the Newhall Gardens, just off Newhall Road (see page 55).

Amongst his greatest feats were: the 6-days race held at the Agricultural Hall in Islington in 1880 when he won first prize by walking 406 miles, his race against a horse and trap for nearly 20 miles between Tinsley and Doncaster in 1884 (he lost!) and his world record endurance performance at Madison Square Garden, New York in 1888, only beaten in the 1970s. With justification the Kings Head was known at the time as 'The Champion's Rest'.

Cross Attercliffe Road and enter the old parish churchyard (31) through the iron gates. In Church Lane, on the left, a large building (recently demolished) was the garage of A.F. Hancock Limited (32), motorcoach operators, built about 1929. The upper floor, however, was used for a very different form of wheeled transport, being the home of the Attercliffe Palais de Danse roller skating rink for some years. Although roller skates were invented in France in the 18th century, it was only towards the end of the 19th century, after improvements to their performance by the introduction of ball bearings, that this form of skating became popular and accepted as a sport in its own right. A great craze for roller skating swept the United States and Great Britain in the early years of this century and, although this gradually subsided, the sport was still sufficiently popular for this rink to be built in the 1920s. The sprung roller skating floor survived until demolition.

George Littlewood, champion pedestrian, with trophies

Walk through the churchyard to the level area in front of the row of trees. The paving here marks the outline of Christ Church, the first parish church of Attercliffe, which was consecrated on 26th April, 1826 by the Archbishop of York, and replaced the old chapel at Hill Top as the principal Anglican place of worship in the village.

The church, with its 120ft. high square tower was one of the most prominent buildings in

Attercliffe until December 1940, when it was bombed and subsequently demolished. It was designed by the Leeds architect Thomas Taylor (c. 1778–1826), and was one of four 'Million Pound Act' churches built in Sheffield in the 1820s, part of its cost of £11,700 being met from the one million pounds voted by Parliament to reinforce the Established Church in the growing towns of England against the growth of nonconformity. The other three churches in Sheffield were St George's, Brookhill (1825), St Philip's, Infirmary Road (1828) (now demolished) and St Mary's, Bramall Lane (1830). All were built in a distinctive Gothic revival style typical of the period.

The laying of the foundation stone for Christ Church on 30th October 1822, by the Protestant 12th Duke of Norfolk, assisted by the 4th Earl Fitzwilliam (respectively Lords of the Manors of Sheffield and Ecclesall), was an occasion of great celebration. Some 5,000 people attended, including the Master Cutler, the Town Collector, and the Church Burgesses. Afterwards, the Revd John Blackburn, the vicar, provided a meal for several hundred poor people in the field behind the site, now the cemetery.

The stones from the churchyard, which was closed for burials in 1856, have unfortunately almost all been removed, only a few surviving

Sims Attercliffe Garage, later incorporated in Hancock's Garage and the Attercliffe Roller Skating Rink

around the perimeter, their inscriptions forming a record of the lives of former inhabitants.

Follow the path to the gates into Attercliffe cemetery (33). In winter this can seem rather desolate, but at other times it has a surprising sense of peaceful remoteness, and remains an oasis in the heart of the Valley. The cemetery was opened in August 1859. Like most other cemeteries, it was divided into two portions, a consecrated part for those of the Anglican faith, and an unconsecrated part for everyone else. With the parish church being so close however, only a small chapel, demolished 20 to 30 years ago, was built in the unconsecrated part. As the cemetery is quite small (only 4 acres) it was not long before another one was required, and so land at Tinsley Park was purchased and the cemetery there opened in 1882.

Follow the path down to the bottom corner of the cemetery and look over the wall. For centuries the River Don flowed past here in a great bend, below the curving cliff (34) (see illustration on page 10) which gave Attercliffe its name and which is still recognisable

CONSECRATION OF CHRIST CHURCH AND SUNDAY SCHOOL, ATTERCLIFFE, 1826

across to the left behind retaining walls. In the mid 1890s, in one of those engineering feats in which the Victorians excelled, a new, straighter course was created for the river across the neck of the loop, and eventually its original line disappeared beneath Hadfield's Hecla Steelworks which have themselves now partly gone.

Returning to Attercliffe Road notice the stone building (35) with gothic windows on the left side of the churchyard. This was built in 1824, by the National Society as the church school, and it too was designed by Thomas Taylor. It provided accommodation for 120 girls and infants, the boys already having a school on Cocked Hat Piece which was later enlarged to accommodate all the children. This building then became a parish hall. It was altered and enlarged in 1935 and, after the demolition of Christ Church was used for a time as the parish church. It is now a listed building but needs a new use.

Turn left out of the churchyard. On the left are the handsome premises of the Royal Bank of Scotland (36), originally built for the Sheffield and Rotherham Banking Company and designed by the Sheffield architects Gibbs and flockton in 1902. Notice especially the heads on the keystones over the arched windows, the polished pink granite columns, and the fine doors with

GRAVESTONES, ATTERCLIFFE CEMETERY

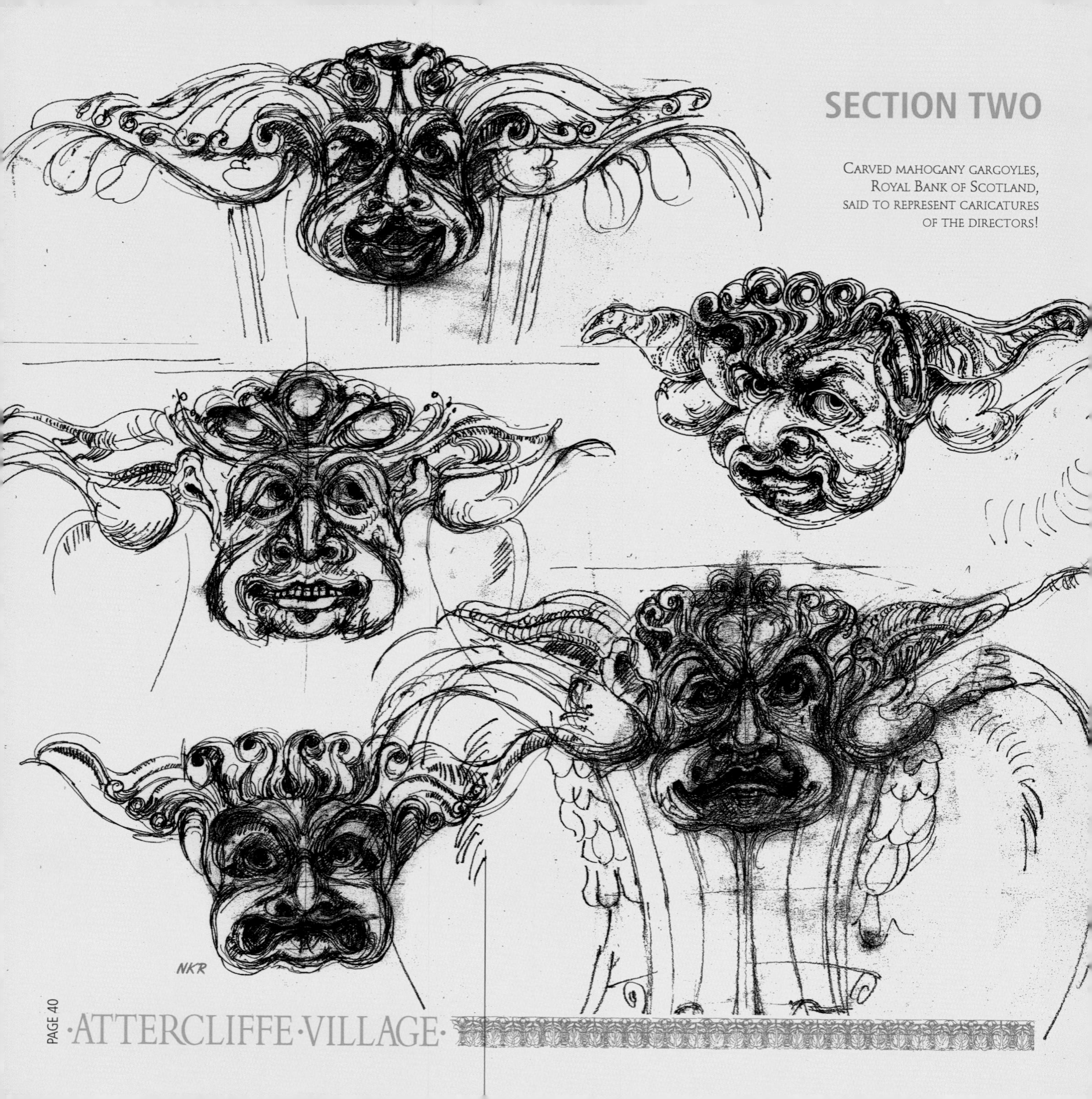

SECTION TWO

Carved mahogany gargoyles, Royal Bank of Scotland, said to represent caricatures of the directors!

Zeenat Restaurant, originally Boots the Chemist

their metalwork and bevelled glass. If the bank is open go inside to look at the largely original interior, which is a good example of Edwardian banking splendour with a carved mahogany counter, mosaic floor and plaster mouldings (see also page 3).

Before the bank a small shoe maker's shop stood here, operated by the eccentric Henry Law. Wearing his old soldier's red tunic, he was a familiar sight in Victorian Attercliffe. His shop also contained his own coffin, which he used as a cupboard until it was needed!

Before crossing the road at the traffic lights, look across to the former pub (37), now a Guest House, which has the date 1901 on its doorway. This stands on the site of one of Attercliffe's oldest public houses, known since 1838 as the Coach and Horses—an appropriate name as the coaches from Sheffield to Rotherham and to Worksop passed here regularly, the latter turning right at the corner to take the road through Darnall.

The building on the corner, elaborately faced in biscuit coloured faience, was completed in 1905 as a branch of Boots the Chemists (38). This familiar firm, founded in Nottingham in 1887, was one of the first with a national network of branches and a 'house-style'. Designed by Boots' architect, A.N. Bromley, this one bears a distinct similarity to the branch in West Street, near Glossop Road Baths, which he designed a year later.

SECTION THREE

WORKSOP ROAD TO ATTERCLIFFE ROAD

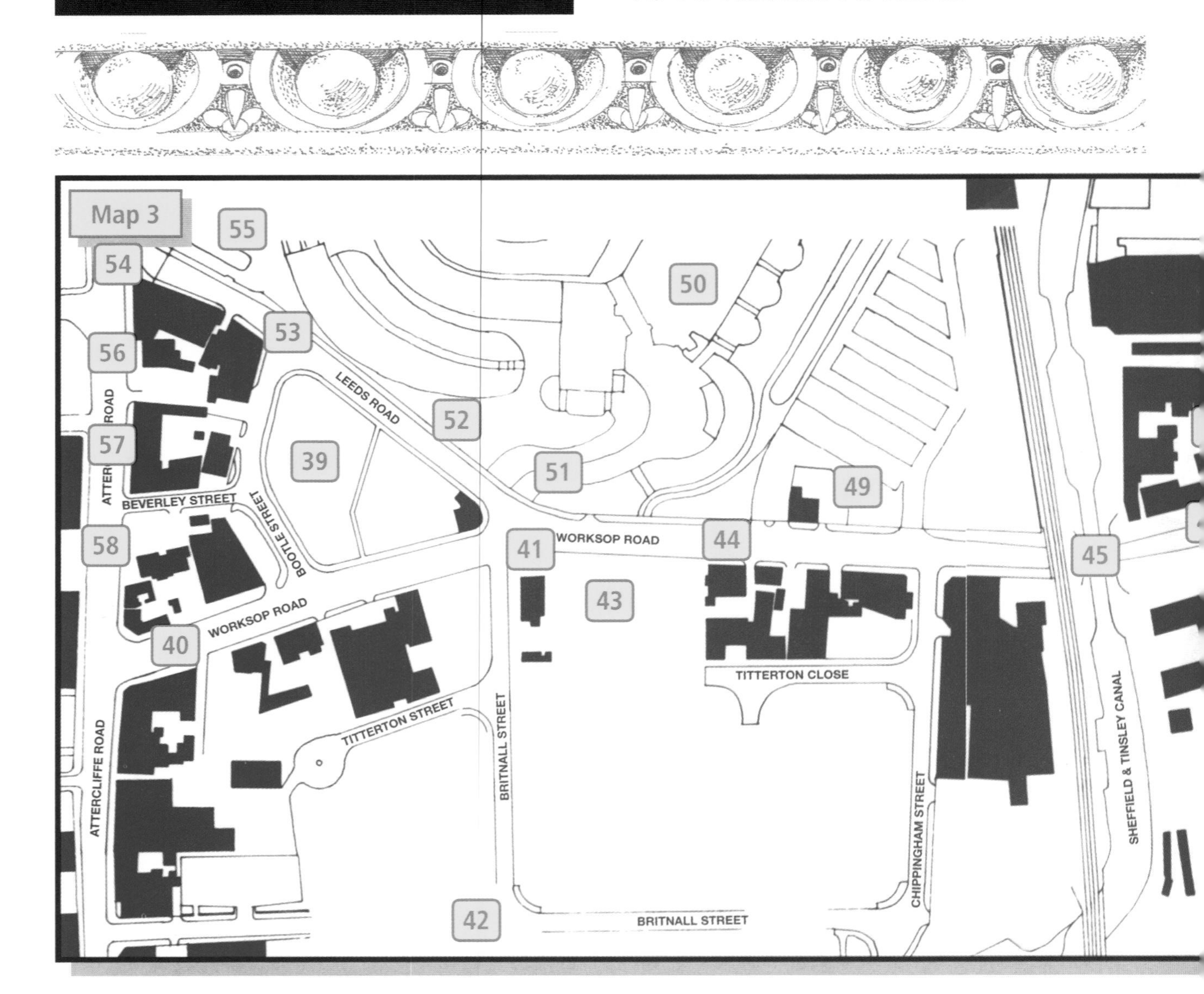

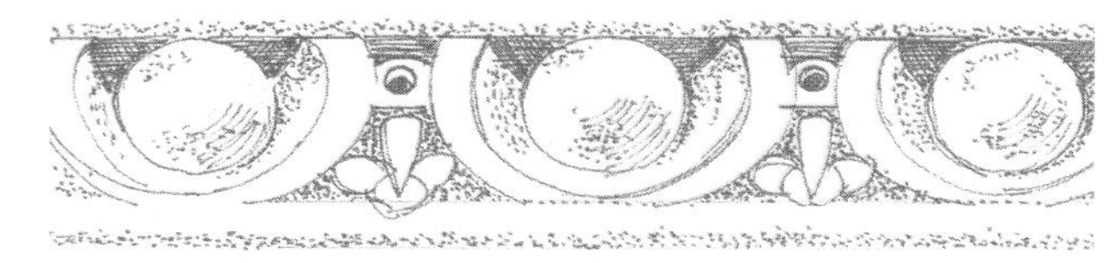

Cross Attercliffe Road and turn down Worksop Road, formerly known as Church Street. Here was the heart of the old village—the triangular area across to the left was called Goose Green in 1637 but later, because its shape suggested the triangular hats fashionable in the 18th Century, became known as Cocked Hat Piece (39). After the Enclosure Act of 1820 it was eventually completely built over. Only in the last few years has part of it been restored, after some 150 years, as an open space, while the pub at the end, built after 1853, preserves its later name, though its signboard is misleading, showing a man with a top hat!

On the right hand side the three-storey Britannia Inn (40) is most striking for the date 1772, in large steel numbers over the gable. There is a long standing tradition that this was where Benjamin Huntsman lived, near to his works, although conclusive evidence has not been found for this. The tradition maintains that the steel date was erected by him. The house itself is earlier than this date but was extended in the 19th century.

Further along, Britnall Street follows the line of a long narrow garden. This had been one of the ancient strip fields and in 1855 belonged to an earlier Cutlers' Arms (41) public house, which used part of it for a skittle alley. At the top of Britnall Street stands a small drop stamp, formerly worked at Ambrose Shardlows. Hammers of this type and larger still operate in works up and down the Valley (42).

SECTION THREE

Beyond the former Cutlers' Arms pub (now Fara's) is one of the most important historic sites (43) in Attercliffe, for it was here that Benjamin Huntsman (1704–76) set up his works in 1770 to exploit his invention of cast, or crucible, steel and laid the foundation for Sheffield's reputation as the quality steel producing centre of the world. He had come to Attercliffe from Handsworth some 19 years earlier, and first occupied premises across the green (where Leeds Road is now), eventually moving to the site where the firm remained for 130 years until it moved to Tinsley Park Road in 1899.

Huntsman was a modest and sober Quaker who had close links with fellow innovator James Watt, perfecter of the steam engine in Birmingham. He is said to have refused membership of the Royal Society—a considerable honour—

Huntsman Works, Worksop Road, early 19th century with crucible shops on right, cementation furnaces left centre and the owner's house and gardens. (Compare with Fairbanks' plan on pages 6 and 7.)

Benjamin Huntsman

WILLIAM HUNTSMAN, SON OF THE INVENTOR, IN TYPICAL QUAKER DRESS. NO PICTURE OF BENJAMIN HUNTSMAN SURVIVES.

because he would not, as a Quaker, swear the necessary oath of allegiance. He founded a local industrial dynasty which prospered not only in steel but in coal mining. Indeed, his great great grandson, Benjamin, was known as the 'Coal King of Attercliffe'. By this time the family had abandoned its earlier dissenting practices and were pillars of the Established Church and Conservative Party, living at Worksop.

In the time of Benjamin's grandson, Francis Huntsman, the works included a fine house with vinery, gardens, fruit walls and coach house, as well as the furnaces, steel house, warehouse and counting house.

The Old Blue Bell pub (44), now closed like so many others in areas where the steel works which supplied their customers have gone, has a rather sedate appearance, enlivened by pilasters of shiny brown faience with swags of leaves and fruit at the top and has, happily, found a new use as a mosque. Its predecessor on the site was once renowned as the meeting place of the legendary 'Attercliffe Stupid Club', a Sick Club whose members had, according to the *Attercliffe Almanack*, to give three months notice if they were going to be ill, and six months before they died. One could only qualify for membership after fishing with a pin in a bucket of water for a day and members had to attend meetings wearing their coats buttoned up back to front!

Walk towards the railway bridge and the great stone aqueduct (45) built in 1819 to carry the canal over Worksop Road. The steps on the right once led up to Attercliffe Station, originally opened in 1868, on the MSL line made to link Victoria Station with Tinsley and ultimately Barnsley. It closed in 1927. The railway was one of the reasons why Brown Bayleys chose to site their steelworks on the land immediately to the north-west in the 1870s, as it provided the ideal means of receiving raw materials and despatching their finished products (chiefly railway rails).

Worksop Road and Darnall Road in the 19th century linked the two villages of Attercliffe and Darnall; the boundary being marked by a tollbar. Along its length were a number of early industrial enterprises. On the left was Makin's Attercliffe Steelworks (46) and beyond that the Attercliffe Pottery (hence the original name of Coleridge Road—Pothouse Lane). On the right hand side, where Sanderson Kayser's steelworks now stands, was a glassworks.

At the corner of Wilfrid Road stands an almost complete Victorian steelworks (47), including timehouse, office block and two melting shops, dating from 1872, with 48 and 84 melting holes respectively. These enabled large items to be cast, using a small army of skilled melters, and was last used during World War II. They are now unique in Britain and are both Listed Buildings Grade II*. It is hoped that they will soon be open to the public and in use once again for a variety of community enterprises.

By the side of the Darnall Road is Kirk Bridge Dyke (48), a small and unfortunately polluted stream which eventually flows into the River Don, and which for most of its course is now channelled underground. The wall itself is of interest because the hard and sharp-surfaced lumps on the top are made of 'crozzil'. This was the airtight 'crust' placed over the top of the 'coffins' containing iron and charcoal when producing steel in conical cementation furnaces (see picture below). It was made of clay and wheel swarf (from cutlers' wheels) and during the long firing of some three weeks was baked hard. At the end of the process it was broken up so the steel and charcoal could be removed and, in the best tradition of 'waste not want not', was often used as a coping for walls.

Returning under the aqueduct and along Worksop Road, note the former White Hart Inn (49),

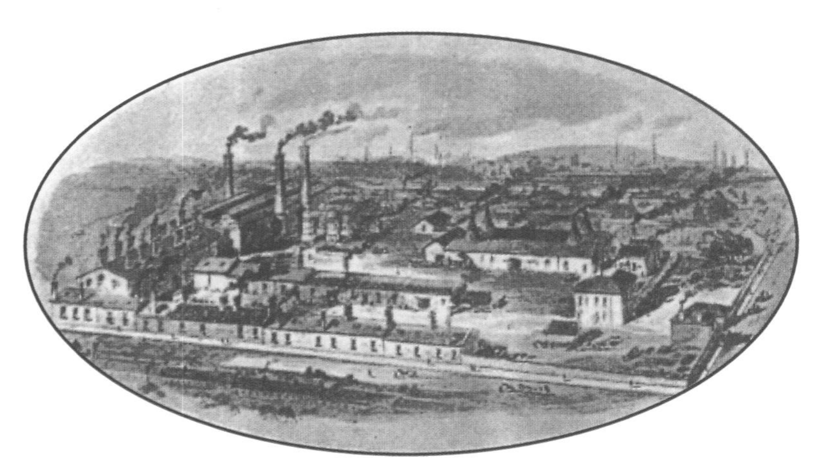

Darnall Furnaces, 1871. Many of these buildings survive intact on Wilfrid Road.

Detail from Blue Bell

which stands on the site of an older public house of that name. In 1819 it adjoined a bowling green, providing a more sedate form of recreation than the skittle alley behind the Cutlers' Arms.

The most prominent building on Worksop Road now, is the Don Valley Sports Stadium (50). This is by no means the first athletics track to have been built in Attercliffe (see page 55), but now replaces what was one of the East End's largest steelworks, that of Brown Bayleys, which employed thousands. Founded in 1870 as Brown Bayley and Dixon, it was the cause of some controversy since Sir John Brown was associated with the new enterprise, despite having agreed not to set up in competition with his old firm, John Brown's, nearby in Savile Street, when he retired.

The firm's most famous employee was Harry Brearley, the inventor of stainless steel, who ran the works in the inter-war

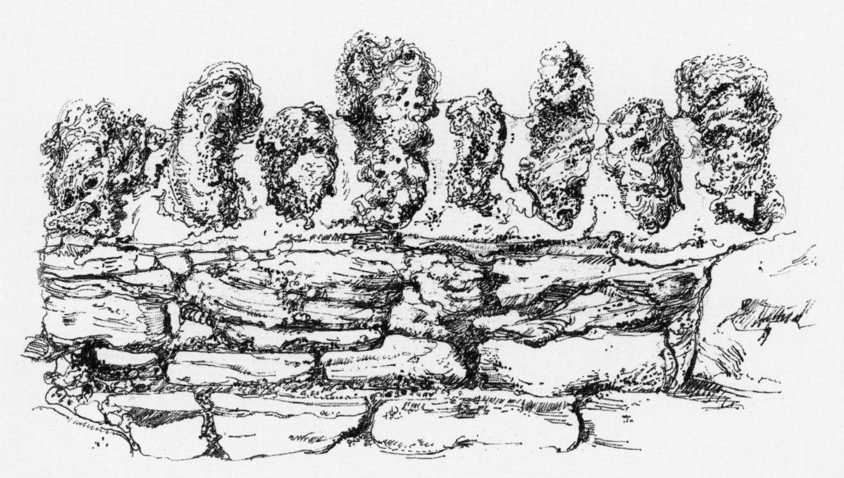

Wall topped with 'crozzil', a furnace byproduct

Harry Brearley (1871–1948), inventor of stainless steel

Brown Bayley Steels, catalogue (right).
A modern-day view of Don Valley
Stadium (main picture).

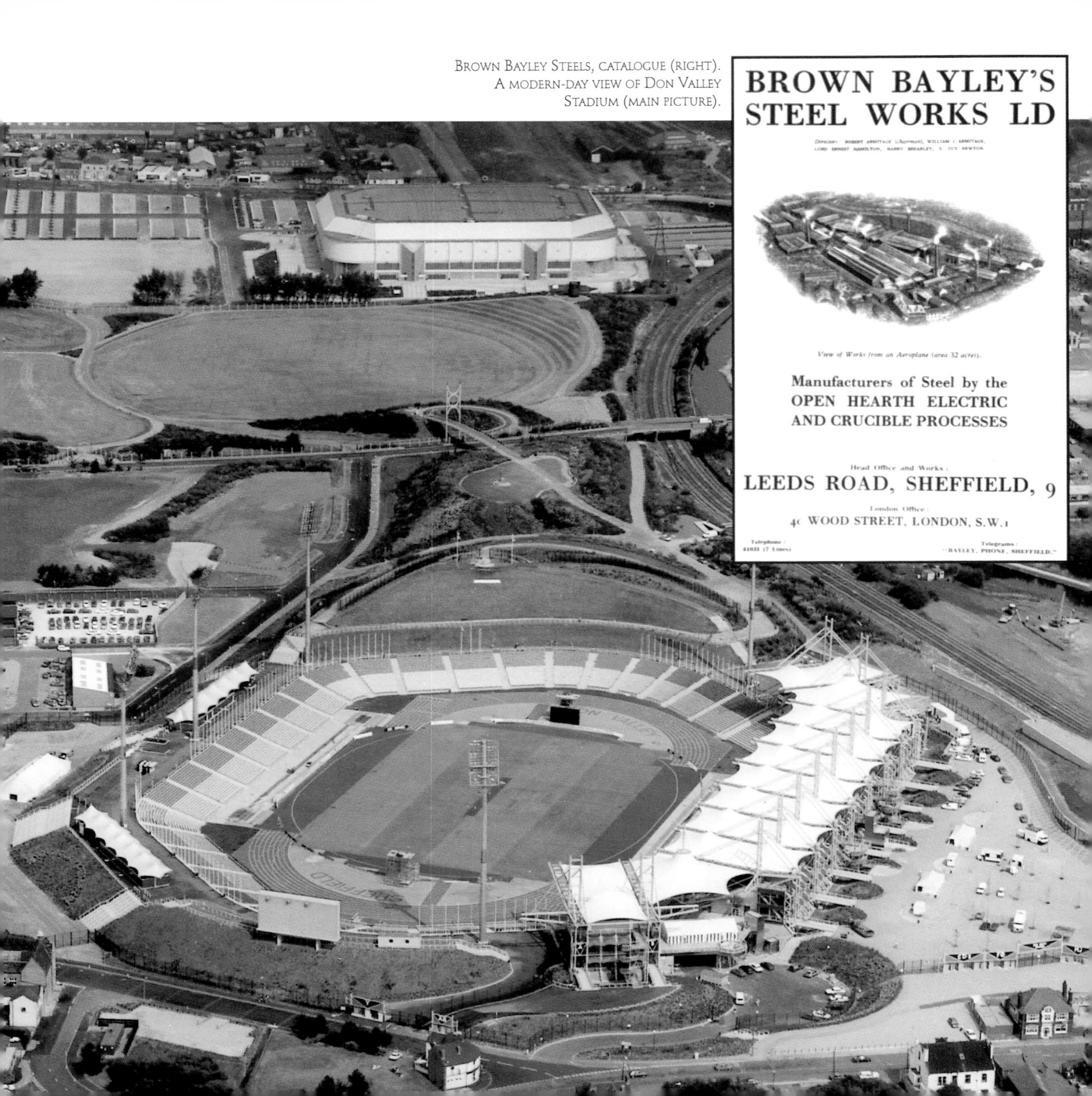

period, again after a bitter dispute with Firth Browns Ltd. In 1930 and 1931 the firm supplied the stainless steel chain collar used to strengthen the dome of St Paul's, which is sometimes credited with the dome's survival of the London Blitz. The company also specialised in railway axles, wheels and springs.

Brown Bayleys ran an unusual fleet of steam powered lorries which were a familiar sight in Attercliffe well into the 1960's. One is now on display in the Glasgow Transport Museum with its original Brown Bayley livery.

The works also had fine offices (51), opposite the Cocked Hat pub, designed in the Queen Anne style in 1911 by the Lutyens-inspired architect, A.F. Royds.

Brown Bayleys became part of Hadfields in 1978 then closed down in 1981, demolition of the works being completed in 1986.

The large hill behind the Don Valley Stadium set in the East End Park, was constructed partly using the piles of concrete from the foundations of the old works.

Next to the former works offices on Leeds Road was the Friends Adult School (52). A school was started by the Society of Friends, or Quakers, in 1884. The building was opened in 1903, and comprised a schoolroom on the ground floor, and recreation room and temperance bar in the semi-basement. The non-sectarian classes, held in the evenings and on Sunday afternoons, were open to all adults wanting to learn to read and write.

BROWN BAYLEY STEAM LORRY

There was also a Sick and Funeral Club, and Savings Bank, all members having an equal voice in their management. The school represented one of the earliest adult education initiatives in the city.

The temperance bar was not the first of its kind in Attercliffe, for Ralph Skelton, Councillor for Attercliffe from 1862 to 1877, had founded a Temperance Society in a building on the green in 1855. Earlier than this, in 1845, a Temperance Hotel existed in the village, while in 1879 the Attercliffe Temperance Hall was established in Beverley Street. Such activities and enterprises are not surprising in view of the strength of nonconformity in the community and the large number of pubs!

Almost opposite the site of the Adult School was the first village school, erected by public subscription in 1779. After being adopted by the National Society it was closely associated with Christ Church and, together with the girls' and infants' school in the churchyard, was the only local school of any size until Huntsman's Gardens opened in 1884.

The brick building on the corner of Beverley Street and Leeds Road (53) was Attercliffe Public Library, designed by the City Surveyor, Charles Wike, and opened on 11th August 1894 by the Mayor. It was the fourth branch library to be built in the city and replaced the temporary premises in Attercliffe House nearby. Its completion was the culmination of a long campaign by local people for a library, vigorously supported by the *Attercliffe Almanack*. The stone carvings over the doorway and in the three gables, and the elaborate rainwater head on the corner, are worth closer examination.

Adjoining it is Attercliffe Baths (54), opened on 15th May, 1879, and closed in the early 1980s. The building is rather curious in having corner bays built in stone, while the rest is of brick with stone dressings. The baths was a popular place for public meetings and political gatherings in the early years of this century. In addition to swimming, the building also housed 'slipper baths' used regularly by thousands, who lacked a bath in their own house, up to the 1970s. Both of these buildings have been saved from demolition and are now used as offices.

Running down the North side of the stadium, is Old Hall Road, which commemorates

FORMER ATTERCLIFFE LIBRARY
(NOW STADIUM CORNER)

one of old Attercliffe's most important buildings of which nothing, alas, survives today (indeed part of it was demolished in 1868 to allow this road to be made). Attercliffe Hall (55), known later as the Old Hall, to distinguish it from nearby New Hall, was certainly in existence by the late 16th Century, and was probably, in origin, much older. It belonged to one of Attercliffe's leading families, the Spencers, who helped to build Hill Top Chapel and supported the Parliamentarian cause in the Civil War as a result of which the Hall was sacked by Royalist troops and Colonel Spencer imprisoned for a time.

It was at the Hall and at the invitation of the Spencers, that Richard Frankland, a leading nonconformist minister, set up an academy in 1686. He stayed for only three years but the college was revived in 1691 by Timothy Jollie, minister at Upper Chapel. There is a also a local, though disputed, tradition that William Walker, who taught maths at the college in this period, was in fact the executioner of King Charles I, and was given shelter by the Spencer family. Walker lived on Darnall Road in a house only recently demolished and he is buried in the Cathedral churchyard.

What is certain, is that for over 50 years Attercliffe Academy, also known as Christ's College, provided an education of university standard, often with a bias towards maths and the sciences, for young men from nonconformist families who were barred from attending Oxford or Cambridge by the Act of Uniformity. Students came from all over the country and included Nicholas Saunderson, the blind mathematician, later Professor at Cambridge, John Bowes who became Lord Chancellor of Ireland, Thomas Secker who later turned to Anglicanism and became Archbishop of Canterbury in 1758, and many other men who were eminent in learning and education in

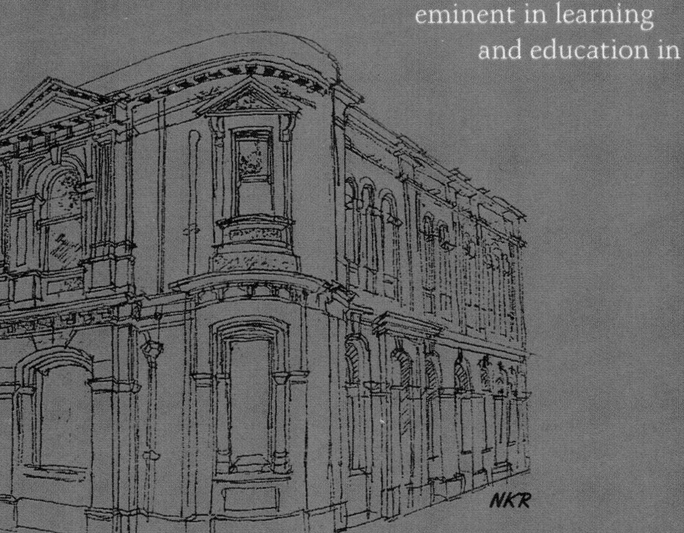

Attercliffe Baths

the 18th Century. After Jollie's death in 1714 the academy continued for some years under his successor, John Wadsworth, but it closed in the early 1740s. The Hall subsided into obscurity and part was later used for manufacturing spades and shovels. The portion of the building which remained after 1868 survived in use as cottages until 1934, when it was demolished by the City Council as unfit, despite attempts to save it on the grounds of its historical associations and its fine 17th-century plasterwork.

Turn left into Attercliffe Road again and walk past the Greyhound pub (56). The houses in the yard behind are amongst the oldest buildings surviving in Attercliffe, probably dating from the early 19th Century, they represent typical artisan dwellings of that time, with one room on each floor.

PART OF ATTERCLIFFE OLD HALL, LATER ATTERCLIFFE ACADEMY, BEFORE DEMOLITION IN THE 1920S

SECTION THREE

The line of small shops (57) beyond the pub dates from 1862. The jewellers shop at No. 796, established in 1895, has a splendid Victorian advertisement for 'Gretna Green Lucky Wedding Rings' to the right of the door, and one wonders what colours might be revealed if the black paint was removed from the tiles below it, as the outline of a flowery pattern can be faintly seen on them.

At the corner is the Attercliffe Liberal Club (58), established in 1881, and opened by A.J. Mundella MP, on 21st October, 1882, at the time when political parties were starting to compete for the votes of working men. The ground floor accommodated a reading room,with the upper floor providing rooms for lectures and meetings. A rival Conservative Club was opened at Carbrook around the same time and was later followed by Attercliffe Radical Club and Attercliffe Non-Political Club (the 'Non-Pots').

ATTERCLIFFE JEWELLERS, ATTERCLIFFE ROAD.

THE REVEREND TIMOTHY JOLLIE (1659–1714), THE INSPIRATIONAL FIRST PRINCIPAL OF ATTERCLIFFE ACADEMY AND MINISTER AT UPPER CHAPEL, SHEFFIELD.

SECTION FOUR

VICARAGE ROAD TO HILLTOP CHAPEL

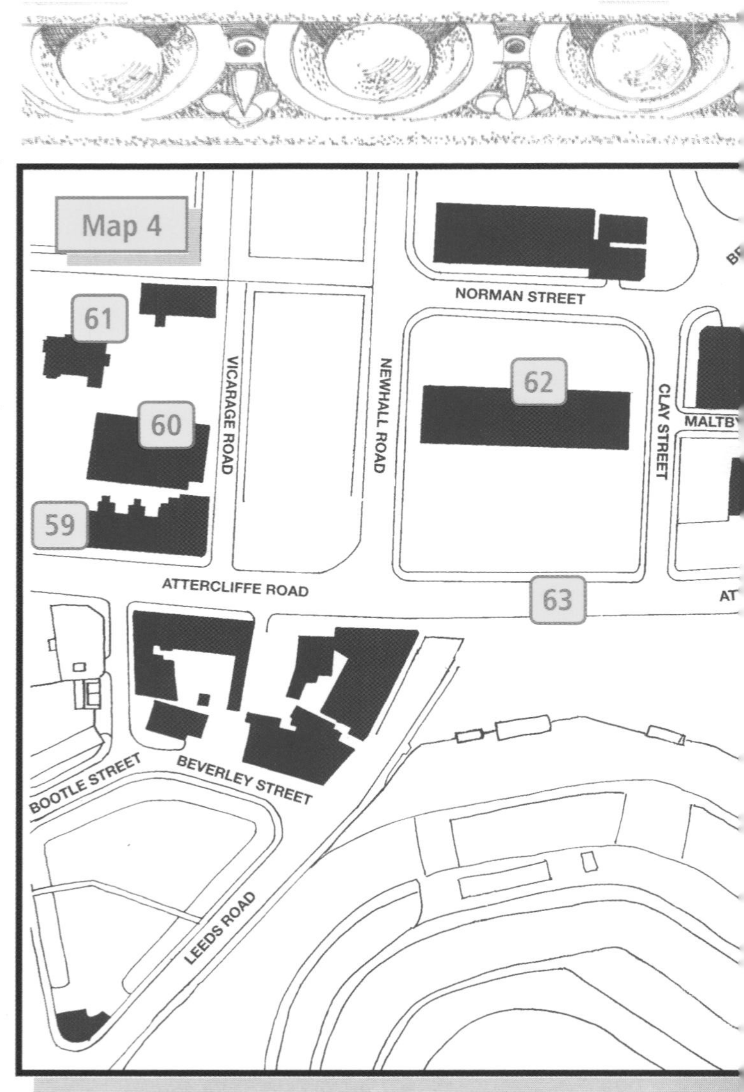

Cross Attercliffe Road to Vicarage Road. On the corner is the second branch of Burtons the Tailors (59), built in 1932 to designs by the Company architect Harry Wilson and, like the first shop on the corner of Staniforth Road, faced in white faience. Notice the small commemorative plaques at pavement level beside the smaller entrances, with the names of members of the Burton family (Stanley Howard, Raymond Montague, Arnold James, and Stephen Austin) and the date on them.

Behind Burtons on Vicarage Road is the Adelphi (60), Attercliffe's third and only surviving cinema, opened in 1920 and closed in 1967, when it switched to bingo. Built in brick, it has coloured glass and faded blue faience decoration and a small dome in the centre front, with a smiling maiden in the keystone. It has recently made a spectacular comeback as a popular nightclub.

Beyond the cinema, the large house, now used as offices (61), was formerly Attercliffe Vicarage; it was built in 1908 to replace an earlier vicarage (see page 58).

Returning to the main road, turn left, and cross over the end of the Newhall Road. This was once a spacious avenue, lined with trees, which led to a large 18th-century house, the New Hall, just across the river in Brightside. It was built in about 1728 by John Fell who ran Attercliffe Forge, but was demolished by 1880 when the garden and grounds became the New Hall Iron Works and streets of terraced houses. Before its demolition, from about 1850 it was used as a hotel and the grounds as a pleasure park, with a

cricket ground, race course, bowling green, maze, lawns and walks, where spectacles such as hot air ballooning, firework displays and concerts drew great crowds. It was also a venue for professional athletics, which drew large numbers to watch and bet on running and walking races in the 1860s and 70s. With champions such as George Littlewood, Sheffield was regarded as the national centre of athletics at this period. There is nothing new in leisure and sporting facilities in Attercliffe!

The land beyond Newhall Road, now an engineering works (62), was famous in the mid-19th century as Rhodes' market garden, celebrated for its rhubarb. Later, part of it was the site of Attercliffe's earliest cinema, the Globe, which opened in 1912 and was the fourth cinema to be built in Sheffield. Opposite was the 'Turnpike' public house dated 1868 (63), formerly the Golden Ball, it was the earliest tram terminus when the horse-drawn service to Attercliffe began in 1873.

Continue up to Attercliffe Common, once a rather barren and windswept place some distance from the main village. It was noted as the haunt of highwaymen, of whom the most famous was Spence Broughton whose death is commemorated in 'Broughton Lane'.

On the left, set back from the road, you pass the Attercliffe Vestry Hall (64) built in 1865, and the Vestry Offices built ten years later. On the wall by the front door of the Overseer's House a plaque records that Sir Robert Abbott Hadfield, Baronet, Fellow of the Royal Society, was born here on 28th November 1858, the son of the then

SECTION FOUR

Attercliffe's last surviving cinema building, the Adelphi, Vicarage Road

Overseer. 'World famous as a pioneer in the development of alloy steels', it was under his direction that one of the largest steel companies in the Valley, Hadfields, grew to pre-eminence in special steels for which Sheffield is still famous. A Freeman of the city and Master Cutler in 1899, he died on 30th September 1940. The Overseer's House appears to have been refaced when the present Vestry Hall was built, but the back quarters show the building is older.

The Vestry was a body selected by the rate-payers of the township and in the early 19th century was the only form of self-government for the local community. Its officers, the overseers and rate collectors, were usually respected members of that community, and the Vestry Hall was used for a wide variety of local meetings and events both official and non-official.

The overseer's main job was the payment of Poor Relief to the destitute and unemployed.

The first family planning clinic in Sheffield, the Women's Welfare Clinic, was set up in Attercliffe Vestry Hall in May 1933. Run by the Sheffield Branch of the National Birth Control Association, it was supported by the Women's Co-operative Guild and the Labour Party Women's Section, and was designed to alleviate the burden that frequent pregnancies imposed on working class women in already difficult circumstances. In its first year nearly 2,000 women sought help there.

Next door, on the right, is the old Employment Exchange (65), now a factory, last used

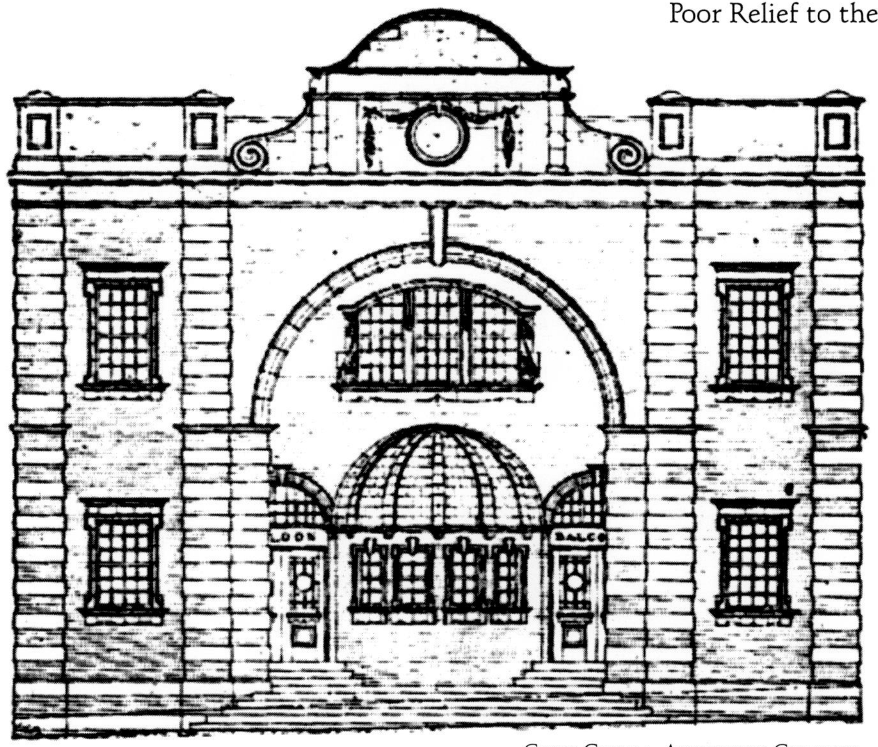

Globe Cinema, Attercliffe Common

THE 18TH-CENTURY VICARAGE OF ATTERCLIFFE, REPLACED IN 1908 BY THE BUILDING STILL STANDING IN VICARAGE ROAD

for payment of benefits during the steel strike of 1981. It was built on the site of the Attercliffe bear-baiting pit—a 'sport' which has now happily entirely died out.

At the top of the 'hill' you reach the oldest surviving building in Attercliffe, the Chapel-of-Ease built in 1629, and known as Hill Top Chapel (66). It was built by a number of local families whose names occur over and over again in Attercliffe's history, to serve the small and then rather isolated community so far from the town centre. The principal people involved were Stephen Bright of Carbrook Hall and William Spencer of Attercliffe Hall, but the Fells, Bamforths, Swallows, Baileys, Staniforths, Sorbys, Milners, Wadsworths, Huntsmans and Shaws are also associated with it at various times. The chapel was opened in 1630, and consecrated on 26th

The Old Attercliffe Bear Baiting Pit was located in an ancient cottage on the Common, demolished in the 1920s. Attercliffe Vestry Hall on left.

HILLTOP CHAPEL, ATTERCLIFFE'S FIRST PURPOSE-BUILT CHURCH, BUILT IN 1630

October 1636. It was restored in 1993 and is now again used for worship and community activities.

The gravestones of many local families can be seen in the chapel yard, the most famous one being that of the Huntsmans, although it seems that the inscription mentioning Benjamin Huntsman who died in 1776 is, contrary to common belief, simply a memorial to him, for rather mysteriously there is no record of him in the chapel burial registers, nor is he known to have been buried anywhere else in Sheffield. This would have marked the edge of Attercliffe Village up until the mid-19th century. The road would then have continued over Attercliffe Common until it reached the small hamlet of Carbrook (see *Five Weirs Walk*, Trail 3).

At this point the trail ends, frequent bus services from the stops opposite the chapel yard will take you back to Washford Bridge, or into the city centre.

Further Information

On Local History

- **Central Library, Surrey Street, Local Studies Library**
- **South Yorkshire Industrial History Society**
  c/o Dora Cottage, Bakewell Road,
  Matlock, DE4 4RB

On Proposals in the Valley

- **Sheffield City Council, Department of Land & Planning,
  Town Hall, Sheffield, S1 2HH**
- **Lower Don Valley Forum, Staniforth Arms Community Pub, Staniforth Road, Sheffield 9**
- **Attercliffe and Darnall Community Enterprise, 678 Attercliffe Road, Sheffield 9**

Further Reading

- ***Attercliffe Almanack*** (Sheffield: Hartley & Son; annually, 1880–1898)
- ***The Story of Old Attercliffe*, George Vine** (Ward Bros, 1936; out of print; available in Local Studies section, Sheffield City Library)
- ***Sheffield's East Enders*, Keith Farnsworth** (Sheffield City Libraries)
- ***Giants of Sheffield Steel*, Geoffrey Tweedale** (Sheffield City Libraries)
- ***A History of Labour in Sheffield*, Sidney Pollard** (Liverpool University Press)
- ***Where Sparrows Coughed*, Frank Hartley** (Sheffield: Sheaf Publishing)
- ***Forging the Valley*, Hay, Olive and Liddament** (Sheffield Academic Press)

There are two other *Sheffield East End History Trails* published by The Hallamshire Press:
No. 1 *The Sheffield and Tinsley Canal*
No. 3 *The Five Weirs Walk*

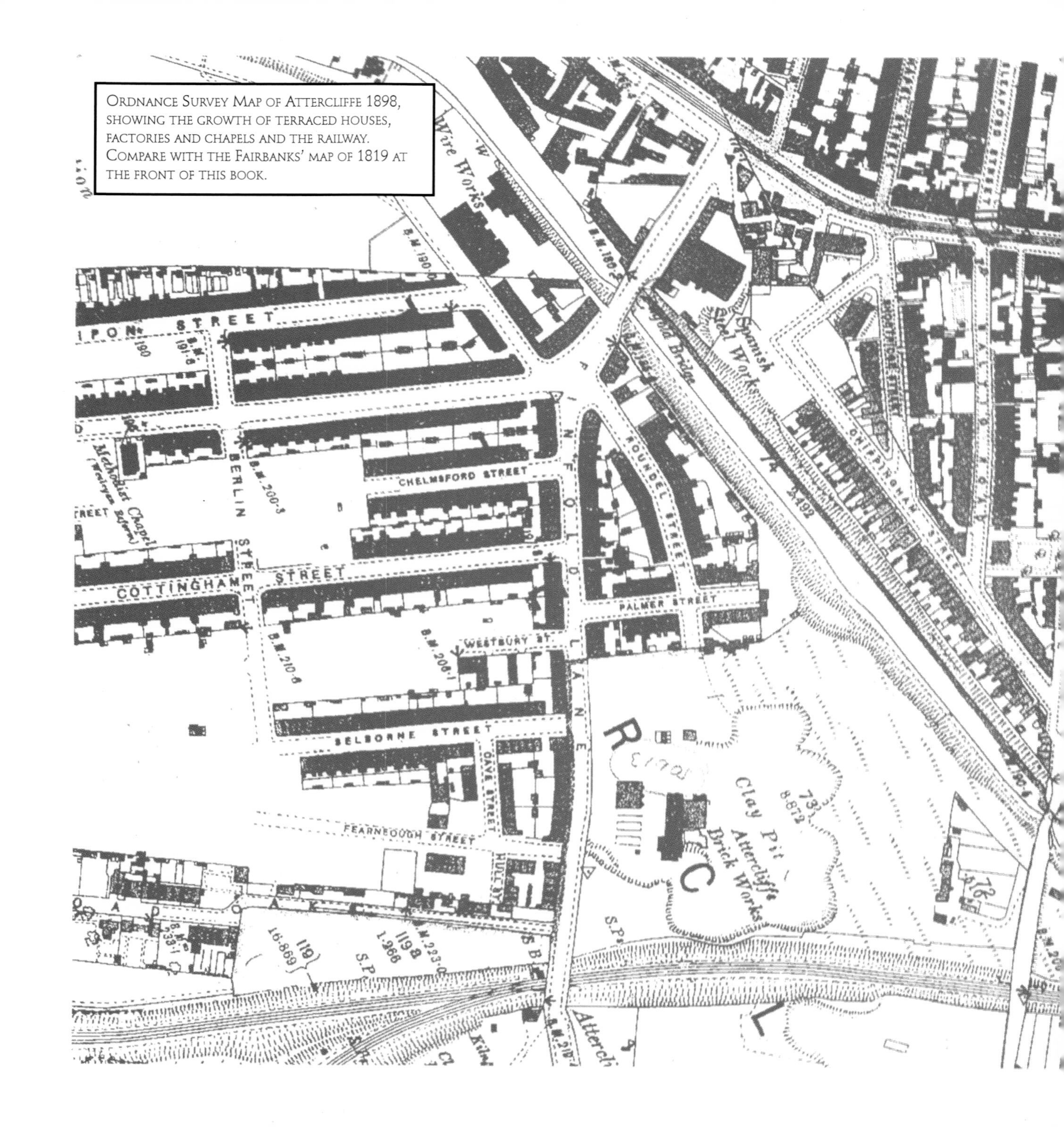

Ordnance Survey Map of Attercliffe 1898, showing the growth of terraced houses, factories and chapels and the railway. Compare with the Fairbanks' map of 1819 at the front of this book.

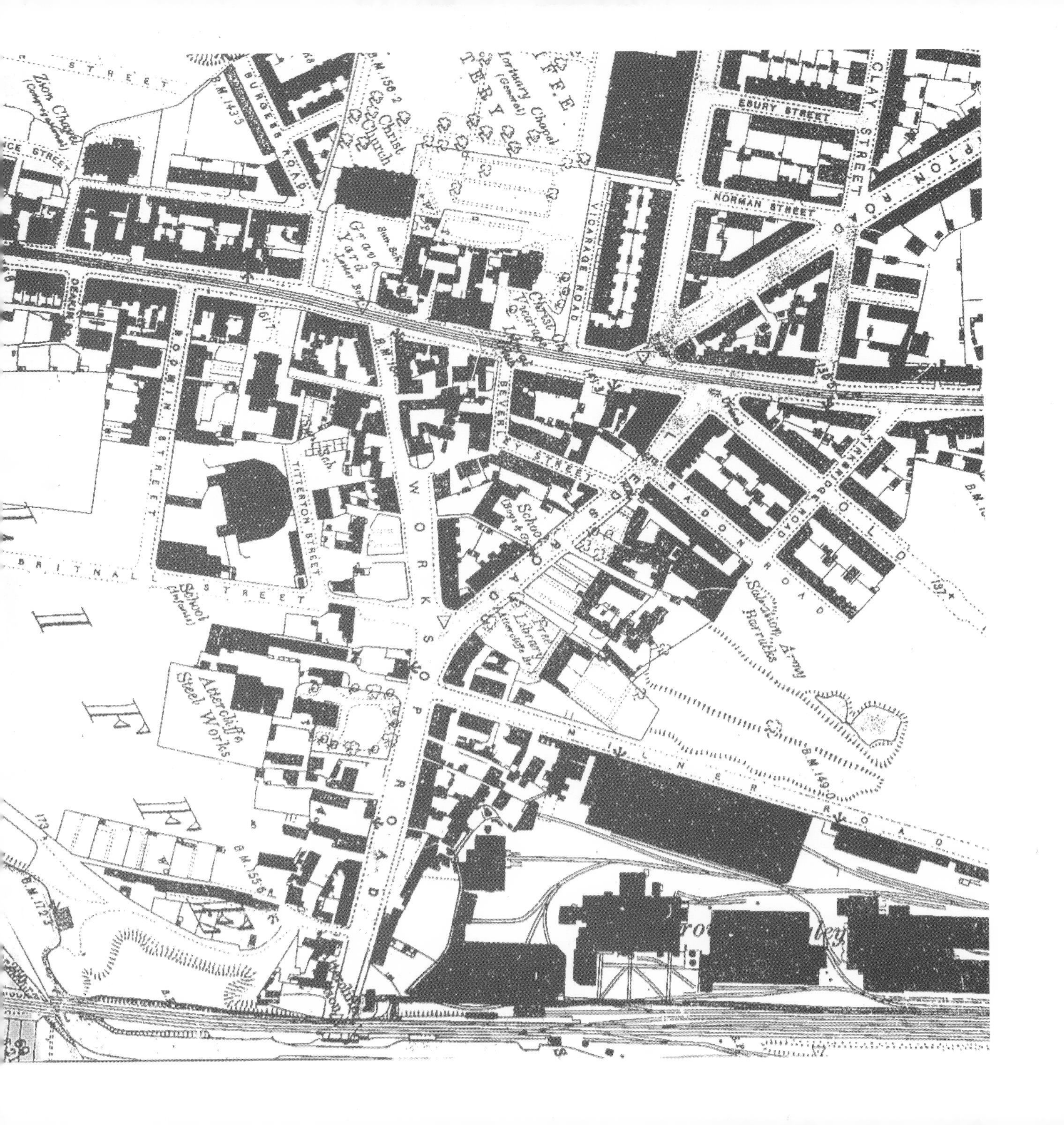

STREET
Zion Chapel (Congregational)
BURGESS ROAD
B.M. 143.5
B.M. 158.2
Christ Church
Mortuary Chapel (General)
EBURY STREET
CLAY STREET
NORMAN STREET
VICARAGE ROAD
Grave Yard
Christ Ch. Vicarage
BODMIN STREET
TITTERTON STREET
BRITNAL STREET
School (Infants)
WORKSOP ROAD
BEVERLEY STREET
School (Boys & Girls)
BEADON ROAD
KIRKBRIDGE ROAD
Salvation Army Barracks
Free Library
Attercliffe Steel Works
MILNER ROAD
B.M. 149.0
B.M. 155.6

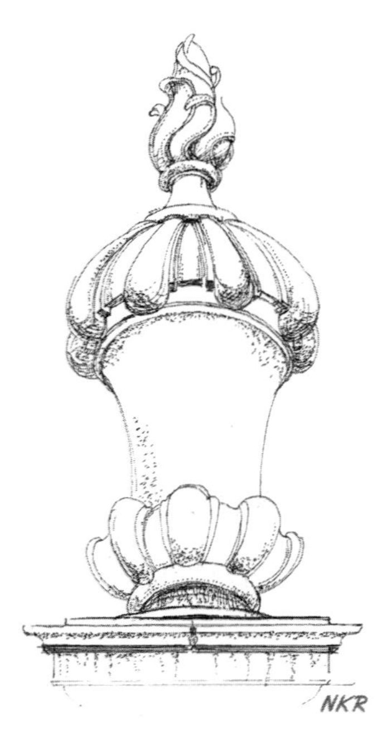

Urn on Banner's roof

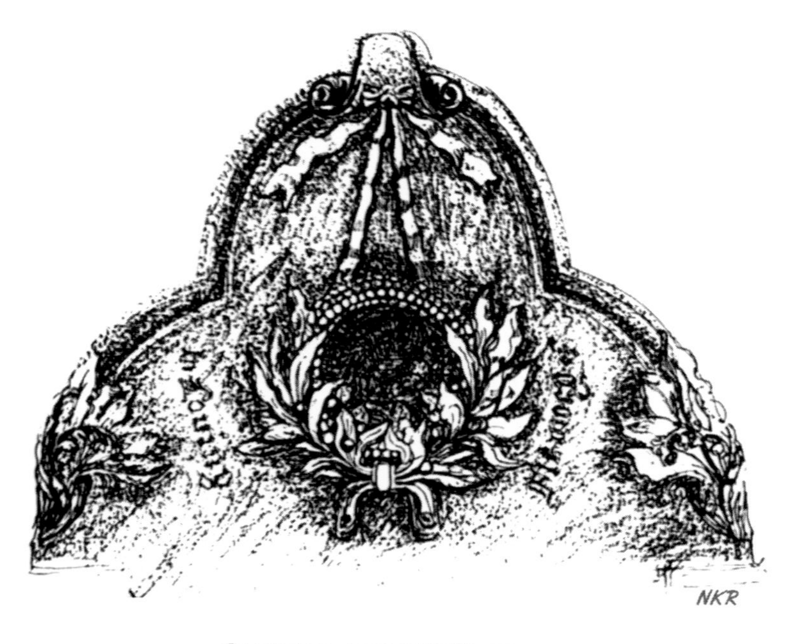

Gravestone, Attercliffe Cemetery

Acknowledgement

The authors wish to thank the Sheffield City Council Directorate of Leisure Services for permission to reproduce material from the collections of the Local Studies section, Central Library and Sheffield Archives.